Routledge Revivals

Man, Creator or Destroyer

First published in 1952, *Man, Creator or Destroyer* makes clear that mankind is preeminent both as a creator and as a destroyer. And we are doomed unless creative man can master destructive man. But how gain this mystery? How strengthen the one and weaken the other? This and other vital questions are answered clearly for the general reader interested in creative work, from art and science to crime-prevention and international statecraft. The first part is concerned with man's creative power which distinguishes him from all else on earth and suggests that man is much more than a machine or an animal. In the second part attention moves to man's destructive power and studies his inclination to obstruct and shatter his own constructive work. The book concludes with an examination of the ways in which the creative power can gain the mastery.

Man, Creator or Destroyer

George Malcolm Stratton

First published in 1952
By George Allen & Unwin Ltd

This edition first published in 2024 by Routledge
4 Park Square, Milton Park, Abingdon, Oxon, OX14 4RN

and by Routledge
605 Third Avenue, New York, NY 10017

Routledge is an imprint of the Taylor & Francis Group, an informa business

© George Allen & Unwin 1952

All rights reserved. No part of this book may be reprinted or reproduced or utilised in any form or by any electronic, mechanical, or other means, now known or hereafter invented, including photocopying and recording, or in any information storage or retrieval system, without permission in writing from the publishers.

Publisher's Note
The publisher has gone to great lengths to ensure the quality of this reprint but points out that some imperfections in the original copies may be apparent.

Disclaimer
The publisher has made every effort to trace copyright holders and welcomes correspondence from those they have been unable to contact.

A Library of Congress record exists under LCCN: 52043233

ISBN: 978-1-032-74777-4 (hbk)
ISBN: 978-1-003-47084-7 (ebk)
ISBN: 978-1-032-74778-1 (pbk)

Book DOI 10.4324/9781003470847

MAN
CREATOR
or
DESTROYER

GEORGE MALCOLM
STRATTON
B.A., California; M.A., Yale;
M.A. and Ph.D., Leipzig
Professor of Psychology in the
University of California
Member of the National Academy
of Sciences

*

London
GEORGE ALLEN & UNWIN LTD
RUSKIN HOUSE · MUSEUM STREET

FIRST PUBLISHED 1952

This book is copyright under the Berne Convention. Apart from any fair dealing for the purposes of private study, research, criticism or review, as permitted under the Copyright Act 1911, no portion may be reproduced by any process without written permission. Enquiry should be made to the publisher

PRINTED IN GREAT BRITAIN
in 12 point Granjon type
BY HEADLEY BROTHERS LTD
109 KINGSWAY W C 2
AND ASHFORD KENT

To A.E.S.

PREFACE

THE present writing considers carefully the oft-repeated assertion that man is nothing but a helpless particle in an immense universe; or is only a machine, or only an animal. Instead the writer finds in man a creative power revealed in his novel productions, not only in the material world, but also in our social surroundings and in our own spirits. Not only do men create railways and airways, factories and commerce, but still more—and beyond all other creatures we know—do men bring into being laboratories and libraries, hospitals, theatres, and observatories; with new obligations, aspirations and worship.

Attention then moves to man's power to obstruct and shatter all this constructive work. The source of this use of his ability is sought out and described, along with that of his power to upbuild. And the ways are indicated by which from the same wasteland of human nature both of these opposites come forth, with the constructive power, if he will, given mastery.

The writing is intended for the humanely interested general reader; its thought keeps close to visible, concrete facts while yet aware of the depth and height of what is not reached by science alone.

In many ways it is, so far as the author is aware, a new treatment of the creative and the destructive aspects of human life, and he believes it meets constructively much that is so negative in the critical thinking of to-day.

ACKNOWLEDGMENT

THE author wishes to acknowledge his debt to several individuals and to thank them heartily for their personal assistance.

Miss Marie Grote (Mrs. Carl A. Larson), a former student of his, at his request, wrote him an account of a Japanese infant fostered from birth to adulthood by Whites. While living in Hawaii, Miss Grote had become well acquainted personally with the young Japanese woman and her history. My own account is based on that of Miss Grote's, with her kind permission.

Professor Stephen S. Visher of Indiana University, in answer to an enquiry, generously sent a number of reports of his researches indispensable for the understanding of this subject. These had not been available to the writer. Thus it was possible, on p. 53, to speak assuredly concerning the parentage of many prominent Americans.

In preparing the lists of nations on p. 103, the writer received great help from colleagues learned in history, especially Dr. Palm, Dr. Kerner and Dr. King. But if, after this care, there should be any important errors in the lists, the writer alone is responsible.

CONTENTS

	page
PREFACE	vii
ACKNOWLEDGMENT	viii

THE FIRST PART

Creators

I MAN BELITTLED, AND HIS REPLY
- 'Man is Nothing But . . .' — 3
- Men Transform their Habitation — 6
- Men Reshape their Social Setting — 9
- Men Make Themselves Anew — 12
- 'Men are Only Machines' — 15
- The Animal in Man — 17
- Contrasts between Men and Animals — 20
- The Eminence of Man — 25

II LARGE REQUISITES FOR EXCELLENCE
- A Geography of Talent — 32
- Indispensables for Creative Power — 36
- The Encompassing Community — 41
- A Hermit of the Sierra — 46

III FROM APPRENTICESHIP TO MASTERY
- Plowing and Seedtime — 50
- Town and Countryside — 55
- Insight after Baffled Effort — 58
- Favouring Winds and Hurricane — 62

IV CREATIVE POWER ITSELF
- Ingredients of Ability — 69
- Diverse Complements of Talent — 74
- The Attachments and Purposes of the Man — 79

CONTENTS

THE SECOND PART

Destroyers and Creators

		page
V	ABILITY TURNS DESTRUCTIVE	
	Dishonour in the Homeland and Beyond	87
VI	AN EXPEDITION AND ITS OUTCOME	
	Conflicting Reports by Earlier Explorers	90
	The Headwaters of Turbulence Within the Nation	95
	The Terrain of War and Peace	102
	The Worth of What We've Found	110
VII	THE WILDS AND THEIR RECLAMATION	
	Men's Nature when Unreclaimed	116
	Aims of the Reclamation	122
	The Ways of the Dynamic Process	128
	Success and Failure Within Nations	133
VIII	RECLAIMING THE INTERNATIONAL MIND	
	The Mind that Still Prevails	140
	Misshapen Offspring of that Mind	144
	Forms Emerging from the Mist	147
	The Mind that Must Be Achieved	150
	How to Achieve this Mind	156
	The Greatest of All Arts	161
INDEX		167

THE FIRST PART

*

Creators

I

MAN BELITTLED, AND HIS REPLY

'MAN IS NOTHING BUT ...'

I

THE creative powers in men have always contended with what is destructive in him. But in our present age this conflict has reached a magnitude our world has never known before. It rages in multitudes of individuals and families, between classes, in races, and both within nations and between them. The struggle appears in social life and morals; in the economic and political life, in literature and painting, and in all else that speaks of the outer and the inner world. The greatest nations now know that a world in ruins awaits them unless they avert this calamity with all that is in them of knowledge and wisdom and will. Their minds, under God, must be their help. And yet at the very hour when only mind can save us, science—as though it were the cynic intellect in *Faust*—suggests the futility of all the thought and striving of men's minds. To many we seem but leaves whirled and borne aimlessly by gusts of the world's wind.

Science, it is true, has not authoritatively and beyond appeal, pronounced such a judgment upon us. It is, rather, that certain revolutionary discoveries about man suggest this verdict—while not declaring it outright. And many persons, scientists, even—for they, too, are suggestible, and science has its styles, its fashions—accept this intimation, and count it proven truth that men are helpless in the tide of world events.

We should now glance at some of these aspects of science which keep many from confident effort to achieve high purposes, the objects of men's deep desires.

II

One morning soon after the explosions of atomic energy over Japan had stricken the world, I met a friend, an astronomer, on a path leading through pine and redwood from his observatory. Witlessly I asked him what the stars were thinking of us. 'We and our earth,' he answered, 'are nothing but a mote in their immensity. They have no interest in us.' Like many to-day and in the past, he was repeating the thought: 'When I behold the heavens—what is man!'

This impact of astronomy is trebled by that of other sciences, and especially of those scientists whose undoubted conclusion is, that man is nothing but an animal among animals, among the highest of them, it is true, but yet of the same order with marmosets and lemurs, with monkeys and with apes. His frame is like theirs, and in him are organs like theirs, and functioning like theirs. And he, like all other animals, indeed like all living things on earth, has appeared on the scene as the result of the slow process of evolution. As with all the animals, so with him, there has been the struggle for existence, and the survival of the fit; and by heredity there are transmitted those characteristics which contribute to the fitness. The environment thus indirectly presses men as well as animals into conformity with their physical surroundings. Facts like these cause many to dismiss with a shrug and to regard as a fable any hint of man's power and worth: 'A fly sat on the axle, and cried, "See what a dust I raise!"'

III

Thus far we have been hearing from the sciences whose concern is chiefly with inanimate nature, and with animals below man. What of the scientists who give special heed to man's mind? Do these not offer a quite different report, assuring us that man, after all, is no weakling; is indeed in no small measure the master of his fate?

Yet in truth the prevailing minds from this quarter are no less wintry toward any but the humblest claims for man. To-day many scientific students of mind arrive at their conclusions by way of the manifestations of its disorders, and its appearance in rats and other animals. And for these specialists, the result is, that our psychic life is either swept aside entirely or else is 'functional', serving the bodily life of man and consisting mainly of certain biological drives—of hunger and thirst, for example, and of pugnacity and sex—serving to maintain the individual and his kind. The mind, they hold, exists to serve these needs. Its action throughout life is fairly restricted to this menial service.

Other specialists, whose approach to the mind is by way of the nervous system, find here the key to our psychic life. Poison the brain by alcohol or other drugs, and derangement runs through judgment, emotion and purpose. A wound to the infant's brain may bring life-long mental defect. An insult to the nervous system deep enough, ends all conscious life. With so much known, many of these specialists conclude that, were all known, the nervous system, the glands and blood-stream, and all that affects these would completely account for all we do. Such men are apt to hold that the mind itself is no originating and responsible source of action in the physical world about us. Our conscious life in truth appears to them to be but a mysterious accompaniment to certain physical events. The acts of the living body are thus regarded as automatic acts, 'mechanisms' in great variety, of which the knee-jerk is a familiar example. According to this view, man is nothing but a machine—endlessly complex, it is true—but a machine, an automaton.

This, and the other conclusion—that man is only an animal—often seem established facts, like gravitation and the earth's course around the sun. The consequences of such beliefs are grave indeed. For if man be only a machine, he cannot rightly be condemned if he crushes down all that is in his way as ruthlessly as does a steam roller working on a road. Or if he be only an animal, should he be blamed for springing on his living prey and rending it as does a tiger? Moral obligation, moral responsibility, moral dignity would here have no place; and man would be stripped of much of the worth commonly recognized as his.

IV

It should not be thought, however, that the belief of many scientists proves it true that man is an animal and nothing but an animal, and that his mind at most fulfills an animal function, and is of no larger consequence than this.

In the following chapters there will be no attempt to reject anything that competent investigators are agreed upon; but rather to supplement it, by setting forth what, it is thought, may encourage denial, and may encourage the counter-belief that, with all our kinship with the animals, we have also the marks of a different kinship—shown not only in such powers as meet his animal needs, but also in creative power of a degree and quality which does not appear in even the highest life below that of man.

We should study the evidence for and against the low estimate of mankind's ability, and examine a very different appraisal—that men have it in them to become either effectual or inert, to become here immeasurably creative, and there destructive beyond all bounds; and that besides these two opposites, man also has it in him to become as driftwood at sea. And then if men actually are all of these things at once, it will be important indeed to see what we can of the sources of these amazing divergences of outcome in human life. Then we can with more confidence set our hands to have in this world of ours what all men of goodwill now earnestly desire.

This is not a matter only for the pale student. It touches the moment's urgency—and may combat for many the impulse to flinch from what our time demands of us, flinch from saying: 'No, all this is beyond our powers, beyond the power of all mankind.' Instead, it is hoped that they may with intellectual confidence call upon themselves and one another to play the man.

MEN TRANSFORM THEIR HABITATION

I

Men are re-making their physical habitation. Earth and air, plants and animals, are taken in hand and brought nearer to human liking. In this he is a creator, not by bringing forth out of nothing, but by changing what is around him into what suits his use and pleasure.

Thus the plain and upland, under his hand, are plowed and harrowed. He requires the swamp and desert to produce for him grasses and grains and fruits more suited to his use than nature ever offered him. The forest is felled for his housing, and to yield pasture for such animals as have been changed from wild beasts into servants. Man bridges the river or dams it; he tears down a mountainside to fill a gorge for his road and railway; he makes dry ground into a watercourse between river and river, lake and sea, between ocean and ocean. A few soldiers and later a few priests come to a barren shore, and soon there is a city with its dwellings and shops, and warehouses; its school-houses and steeples, its parks and museums. Pure water is made to flow in from distant sources, and at night the darkness can at will become light.

II

But the passing of man's natural habitat of cave or rocky overhang, into hut or cottage, the countryside into farm, then into village and metropolis is not all. He not only re-shapes what he has long possessed, but he also extends his domain in all dimensions. He lengthens his reach and grasp. With enginery of his contriving he reaches down into depth below depth; and as from his basement brings up coal, oil and gas; brings up iron, copper and tin.

And even as canoe or ox-cart enlarged man's old-time habitation adding novelties to what he had before touched and seen, so in time other inventions of his, now whisked him—mind, body and possessions—across continents and oceans, by earth, sea, and air, so that San Francisco is suburban to New York, both to London, Moscow and Bombay. The man who inhabits one dwells in all.

Even farther, man now can, without moving an inch from farm or village, hear what is said and done at the ends of the earth, no longer by some traveller's report, or by mail only, nor by telegraph or telephone, but by radio. This hearing is thus a million-fold nicened, extended, as sight soon will be.

Thus far the enlargement has been by transit, transport, lengthened reach of grasp of ear and eye.

III

But the world that man inhabits is expanded in still other ways, into regions which are not reached by travel or by boring miles down, or by speech brought in by radio. Intellect and imagination go beyond any of these, and give to all who will a share in the knowledge of the earth far below the ocean-floor, below the deepest drilling. We may thus know what happens there to make our whole globe tremble, and what it is that holds aloft the Andes and the Alps.

And in an opposite direction, man by intellect and imagination, gives a new height and majesty to his dwelling-place. He lifts the low firmament beneath which dwelt early man, pushing sun, moon and planets out to distances unthought of before. And far beyond these, we now know are our neighbouring stars and the Milky Way. And out farther still, are star-clouds and clusters at distances from us and from one another which the swiftest known motion, that of light, can cover only in millions of years. These immensities are now included in our known surroundings, for our wonder and to humble or exalt us.

IV

One more dimension of man's enlarged world must not be overlooked in his creative work—that of time, of duration. Time, all time it is true, is a mysterious part of the actual world of the earliest men. Man holds to and makes commonly his own, a stretch of time—past, present and future, far exceeding the actually present instant—with personal recollection, and with collective recall, and record, legend and anticipation. He lives in this larger time, himself and his people. It is of the man's making, supplementing the present, with past and future, even as the space occupied by his body is supplemented by the surrounding spaces which his skin, smell, hearing and sight report to him. Recollections encompass each of us, affecting conduct often more profoundly than does our local habitat.

And for a people, and often for many peoples together, there are events of the past which are retained and transmitted by a collective memory. These are a people's history, tradition, and legend. Amid these they live as among the places and events of to-day. Americans, wherever their homes may be, go their day's round with Lincoln's cabin and memorial in their minds, with Mt. Vernon and Independence Hall, and the shore of Plymouth; even as Britons all round the world are never far from Westminster, Runnymede and from where Norman William landed. These often are more real than much that lies across their street. And so it is with Frank and Dane, with Russian and Chinese. By re-creative memory the past is preserved as a portion of their surroundings.

In this manner, man re-shapes valley and mountain, and adds causeway and bridge, dam and power-line and towered building. Thus he transforms his physical setting. His mental surroundings, his conscious representation of his physical world, has been more astoundingly transformed. For he now consciously conjoins with all this, the lately-won immensity of the heavens, and the duration beyond imagining of life's unfolding on our planet, and of the planet itself before life appeared.

MEN RESHAPE THEIR SOCIAL SETTING

I

Men, as we have just seen, make change on change, in their material surroundings. With no less ardour, do men turn their energies upon their human surroundings, their society, adding to it, subtracting from it. This activity if recalled by instances from the past, as well as by the Titan powers of to-day, reveals our ability to deal almost as we will with ancient and novel customs.

And first, of these changes men bring about in the *extent* of their social connections, in the number of men who co-operate with one another, and in important ways freely act as one. This comes not by nature alone. Only by effort and art conjoined with nature have our great nations come into existence—Great Britain, France, Italy, Germany, Russia, China, Japan and the United States.

And the ability and power of men is displayed not only in the magnitude of this work even in the smallest nations, but also in the variety of their political life. Indescribably fertile have men been, through the ages, in their ways of governing their societies: among various peoples and at different times there have been patriarchs, and there have been matriarchs; the one ruler, and the rule by several together; the voice of the people ignored, or heeded as divine; the laws rigid as flint, and yielding or elastic. Ardour and audacity, master workmanship and imagination have entered into the constitutions by which men have won their hard way out of separate diminutive social units—with only anarchy between them—into governed nations of vast extent. It is an unfinished achievement, yet even now, it reveals the creative power in men.

II

The changes wrought in our social surroundings are, however, more than have just been described. The conduct of individuals within the societies is taken in hand and made less repellent, more acceptable. Certain forms of conduct are prohibited and largely abolished, and other forms are encouraged in their place. Instances of such abolitions and replacements will be of interest.

Human sacrifice was for long a widespread rite in religion. The skulls in thousands—a part of the temples' very structure at certain places in Mexico—bear witness to this practice. The tragic tale of Jeptha's fulfilment of his wild vow; and the story of Abraham's preparation to offer the life of his son Isaac, and sacrificing a ram instead—these and numberless others bear witness to customs now long ended and displaced by more humane offerings.

And, further, blood vengeance, once common, has largely been swept away. Until it was swept away there was inescapable obligation of a man to avenge the death of a kinsman by slaying either the guilty one himself, or someone closely related to him. This custom, this duty, existed round the world. But in time men's minds turned on it sternly, and the obligation to deal with the killer was taken out of private hands and assumed by the wronged family's society. It was now the community's duty to seek out the slayer, determine his guilt, and to punish him. The change in the method of deciding the guilt or innocence of the accused includes the use of many forms of ordeal—filling his mouth with dry rice, by throwing him and his accuser into the Sacred River, by personal combat, and so on—until there was created our modern law court at its best.

This story would make a stirring drama. The whole series of substitutions for savagery and superstition, splendidly illustrates the power of men over their human environs.

Again, men, in co-operation, when there has been a will for the work, have done much to curb the power of the strong to seize what they would of the possession of the weak—*within* many a nation, although not as yet between nations. Instead of taking from him at will the produce of his land and labour or the land itself, there is now established in many a country the legally-guarded right of the weak to part with these goods of his own voluntarily and at a satisfactory price.

And slavery, serfdom and their near kin have virtually ended in all the more civilized countries. In the place of these ancient institutions there is now the right of the labourer to move freely, and with help of a powerful organization of fellow-labourers, to decide under whom he will be employed and at what wages. In time labour's rights will be conjoined with labour's equal obligations to the community as a whole. Men thus are able to sweep away customs and institutions they have come to hate, replacing them with others they approve.

III

Another change in the social setting of individuals is seen in the immense increase men have made in the services they render one another. In primitive societies, it is true, men gave mutual help in war, hunting, and more; but with us to-day men's services are a hundred-fold more varied, more specialized and skilful. And the change has taken place wherever men became civilized, and especially in the Europe, Asia and the Americas of our time. If one should go to any census that tells the full story of the diverse occupations, he will be wonder-struck by the length of the list and by the many names of occupations that to most of us are as strange as the language of the Ifugao.

This entire fabric of assistance that includes all that a civilized man to-day receives from grocer and tailor, hardware merchant and insurance company, scientist and prophet—no tapestry made for an emperor equals a thousandth part of this intricacy of colour and design.

The marvel of men's work upon their physical surroundings, suggested earlier, is thus matched by men's work on their social world. Where men have been willing to fulfil the conditions, they have been able to break many an ancient manacle, and give themselves an enlarged companionship, new rights and dignity, and new power to serve one another.

MEN MAKE THEMSELVES ANEW

The creative powers of man have been illustrated thus far from his transformation of what lies about him—not alone in valley and mountain, in plant and animal, but also in the human life encompassing him, like air and continent.

These, in a sense, are externals, and we must now discover whether man's power here finds its boundary, or, instead, does in fact move freely on, penetrating and extending its transformation into the innermost recesses of the person, his hidden thoughts, the desires of his heart.

I

The actual transformation of man's mind as, I believe, we soon shall see, is not dwarfed when set by the side of his wonder-working in his physical and social surroundings.

There are phases of the mind, it is true, which are as stubborn against man's efforts as, in the physical world, are gravity and the speed of light. But in both realms these unchangeable realities, instead of making creative work impossible, can be made the means and stage of creating.

Men have re-shaped and are re-shaping their interests, their likes, their attachments and affections. And the mind of man is as truly furnished and formed by what he holds dear, as by what he knows.

Now modern life offers, besides the primitive objects of attachment—the mate, the child, the friend, the weapon, the clan and its head—a bewildering variety of other objects.

And with the enlargement of the community, already described, the plain man now cares in some measure for hundreds, thousands, even millions of men of his own nation and beyond. In the United States, more men than ever before are coming to regard the mind and the worth of men across seas, and to feel obligations for their welfare. The one-ness of the world has a new meaning, and gives a new emotional stir.

II

And now of man's purposes—his power to will—into which there enter his knowledge and affection, all wrought into one to make the mind entire. What is achieved here is a further and nearly the most important illustration of mankind's creative power.

For with help from within and without men stand forth whose every ability of intellect and sensibility and impulsion is wrought into a purpose that is incomprehensible to those who have not submitted themselves to a creative discipline. Damien, Schweitzer, and thousands of others of less genius have devoted their all to the well-being of an alien race. Pasteur, the Curies and countless others have given all that was in them to answering, by devices bewildering to the untutored, some questions that for most men would have had no meaning. Woolman, refusing to have in his small tailoring shop any dyed goods, for the dyes came of slave labour, went up and down the land persuading men against slavery, until later there was a multitude led by Lincoln, ready to lay the mighty structure of servitude in ruins. Penn, Smuts, Cecil and Wilson, with all who earlier and later were of a like purpose, began a warfare now in progress against war itself. Such aims as these in control of men are no products of nature; they are works of man's purposive spirit, standing high indeed among the creative works of mankind.

III

Such men as those just considered—Damien, Pasteur and all who have a like humane purpose organizing and commanding their every ability—are, as was said before, nearly the highest manifestations of mankind's creative power.

If so, what are then quite the highest manifestations of that power?

Great communities may rightly be assigned this exalted place. For only in such communities, as later will be seen, are great men possible who in turn foster something of their own spirit in their fellow-members. Every such community is immeasurably more than a large number of separate persons dwelling on a certain extent of land. The detached individuals have been re-made into members of one body, unlike one another, yet prepared for living in amity, holding to certain large ideas and aims in common, and cherishing as their own a continuing company of persons present, past and to come. They lend a hand at changing others into members, and through the years are more and more re-made themselves.

The whole community, like each of its parts, proclaims its defects, its incompletion. Yet, unfinished as it is, this is man's master-work. Many of the nations illustrate this high achievement, giving intelligent, generous, inventive heed to the welfare of their citizens—the chief Scandinavian countries, Switzerland, Czechoslovakia until shattered, the Netherlands, Great Britain, the United States and others to be added by any who attempt a roll of honour. The shame of their defects, which will receive attention later, must not blind one to the splendour of what has here been achieved; and the promise in it of additions still more splendid.

For nation-communities at their best give spur and opportunity to all the fine arts and ten thousand other things of worth, a spur to mutual service and respect and justice. The mosaics of

St. Mark's are little beside such a product. Here fragments of living talent are brought to skill and purpose; are encouraged into slight or strong contrasts of hue and brilliance, and are pieced together into a design unlike that of any single piece. Unlike any mosaic, each living piece here has at least some knowledge of the rest and of the whole, has hidden behind even his discontent, some feeling that he is a part of it, and the living whole is his and has something of his loyalty. This can be said, not of some hope as yet unrealized, but of what is actual and observed in communities of which we to-day are members. The Great Community is the crowning work of the long line of products of creative power—from canals, bridges, and towers that reach the clouds, to the society transformed from savagery, and the individual transformed into legislator, scientist and seer.

Man thus reveals his constructive power, not in some single or narrow field, but in many fields, wide and most diverse. Mightily he works his will in the solid rock, across oceans, and through the air. Fire is his bond servant; he gives new forms and purposes to his social life, and to his own stubborn self. And when, with all this in mind we turn back to the strange affirmations of man's utter impotence—in the opening chapter —those assertions must appear to many of us as belonging to some phantasmic cloudland, where the intelligence forgets all fact and evidence. Instead, man appears in sober truth to be among the great forces of our world, and growing in his mastery of the forces in and about him.

'MEN ARE ONLY MACHINES'

I

As was seen in the opening chapter, many scientists hold that man is essentially nothing but a machine, a collection of mechanisms, run by clever processes of physics and chemistry.

Man unquestionably has much in common with the automobile; with the door that silently opens for us as we approach it; and with radar that penetrates and reports to us what lies hidden in fog or black darkness; and much in common with far simpler machines. For does not the heart drive the blood throughout the body, by means of arteries and capillaries and veins, much as a pump may drive water through some system of pipes. The lungs, too, draw air in, and force it out, to supply oxygen to the blood and carry noxious gases from the blood, like a ventilating system in an office building. The arm swings, lifts and pulls or pushes; jaws and teeth crush and grind quite as does a mill; and so it is in the organs, tissues and cells within our bodies, studied minutely by help of microscope and much else. Ten thousand of our acts are performed without our willing them, or even being aware of them.

II

Since all this and more is now known indubitably, why not go the full length and believe that all acts of ours, even the most intricate and mysterious, were we to know them fully, would be found to be of this mechanical kind, and thus conclude that man himself, through and through, is a machine and nothing more?

The reason why this conclusion is quite unacceptable is that there are stubborn facts that oppose it. For among man's many kinds of action, and in addition to those which clever instruments do, are those of a character we never find in machinery. As an example, no computing machine gives the slightest fragment of evidence that, amid all its intricacies of behaviour, it actually thinks out any single one of these beforehand and intends it, or afterwards reflects on the process, and criticizes it, doubts it, and finally adjudges it as right or wrong. Not the machine but the inventor of the machine does this. He and not the machine, knows the purpose of the instrument, knows the problems of mathematics to be solved, the mathematical steps by which these problems can be solved. The machine is a machine, not a man, and knows nothing of all this; has no need or desire or will for the answers man seeks for his question.

Man, though he has countless mechanisms within him, stands above them, and is possessed of powers and qualities they lack.

He and none of them understands, loves and is loyal. Nor is it likely that machines will soon be advertised that have these in them. And if this should some day actually come to pass—for who can safely prophesy of our human limits—we should be making men, not machines, with choice and will able to rebel and devastate as were the robots in the Czech tragedy. Men who are only machines will not hate and rebel. And if they are not machines and do love and hate, and understandingly adopt and reject, would it not be well to see this clearly, and not speak as though there were no profound difference between machines and men? The difference is real, and few distinctions, particularly in our time, are more heavily laden with meaning. And we shall inevitably be damaged deeply if we fail to be aware of how far our minds are in substance from these tools of ours, and how necessary that this distance be known and honoured.

THE ANIMAL IN MAN

Men have much in them that is mechanical, and yet have much that no machine possesses. Mechanism on mechanism is in us, but we are not machines.

Is not man, however, an animal and nothing more? The zoologists, the biologists—many of them—have no shadow of doubt that we are but animals, and that all who would face reality should accept this as the full truth about ourselves.

This account of man has an endless array of facts in its support, although some persons may venture to withhold their final judgment until they have examined still other evidence. For, while the zoologists tell nothing but the truth about men, yet they do not tell the whole truth. But of this later.

Without delay, then, to a very incomplete story of the many areas of life which men and animals have in common.

I

Each human being and each animal alike begins its life as a minute embryo which contains within it much that later will appear in the mature individual. In this manner we and they come to possess the natural endowment or inheritance that marks each of them and each of us.

Nor is this inheritance similar only in the *manner* of transmission. There are many similarities in what is transmitted, in the *particulars of our endowment and theirs.*

For we and they in common are endowed with organs and the impulses to use them—to breathe, move about, eat and otherwise maintain life amid a strange commingling of threats and promises to existence. We and the animals procreate and die.

Included in this common inheritance is the general resemblance of the human body to that of the higher animals, and especially of those that suckle their young—their bodies and ours alike possessed of a spine, four limbs, a brain and sense-organs and endlessly more.

Also it should here be recalled what was said earlier that man appears upon earth in the course of the same unhurried pageant of evolution in which the animals came upon the scene, with similar lowly antecedents—man having animals not only as his distant and extinct ancestry unhonoured by portraits on his walls, but also by living relatives rarely invited to his board. For among his near animal kin are the monkeys, chimpanzees and gorillas.

And man by evolution came into the same physical environment as did many of the higher animals; and like them he depends upon it for his sustenance; unable to live without breathing its air, and drinking its water, and eating what grows from its soil and sunlight. Like the higher animals he has organs to move about with, seeking and finding these external necessities and by his internal organs drawing from them what is made into tissues of his body.

II

Man and animal alike have come upon the scene and have continued on it by what is called the struggle for existence; by a persistent and successful use of powers to appropriate what is favourable in their surroundings and to escape what threatens.

III

We and the highest animals share also in some powers of mind—not alone in the power of sight, hearing, and all the other senses, but also, in due time, as do dogs and elephants, to attach meaning to what they see, hear, and smell; and eat or reject it; prepare to fight it, or pass it without further heed. Thus they perceive, retain, recognize, and perhaps in some degree dream or imagine, as does the dog asleep by the hearth, who, without waking, makes the beginnings of a growl and a start. Nor can one reasonably doubt that many of the higher animals have their desires, emotions, and aims; experience excitement and fear; anger and attachment; have some mental rudiments of what men have of the restless needs and desires for food, drink, rest, sleep and mating; and of roving forth intent to find what will relieve this disquiet.

Nor will there be many to doubt that higher animals and we human beings have in common no small degree of intelligence, including the power to learn and to solve simple problems. Even rats are notably able to find their food more and more directly and swiftly through an intricate maze. And the classic experiments of Köhler showed the chimpanzee's ability to pile boxes, to climb them and thus get a banana above, which, without the piled boxes, was out of reach; and again, to piece together sticks that could be inserted one in another, to pull into reach a banana on the ground far outside the cage.

Such are but a few of the indications that man and some of the animals have various traits of mind in common.

The highest animals, and animals less high—not to speak of those wondrous creatures the ants and some of the wasps—work together, assist one another in various intricate ways, in herd, or flock or smaller groups as are found among the beavers. They act together, surely in body, and probably in mind also, with insight perhaps into the purpose of the work in which they share; and with some of the companionship, the sympathy that is at the root of human collaboration at its best. Yerkes, in his studies of the chimpanzees and other anthropoids, found ample evidence of sympathy and co-operation.

This far from complete inventory of what is common to men and animals may seem to some an over-labouring of what is obvious. And from this evidence many hurry on beyond and hold that man is an animal and nothing more.

Considerations that to some may suggest doubt of this should next be offered.

CONTRASTS BETWEEN MEN AND ANIMALS

I

Man is in no such subjection to his biological inheritance as are the animals. He has it in him to turn upon his inherited impulses, his 'drives', and to put them in the place he chooses for them. To his natural curiosity, for example, there is given a wider play than that of back-fence gossip, taking it into history, and natural science. His natural rapacity is, for most of us, transmuted into trade. And, sex, for the more civilized is deflected from its natural course into marriage, with concern for the mother of the children; while natural pugnacity is so transformed in our civilized communities, that almost all members settle their serious disputes, not by combat and killing, but by various devices of pacific settlement, including police and trial in court of law.

Animals, in contrast, show no such power over their inherited impulses. They accept them and obey them as best they can.

II

Men possess in overflowing measure another kind of heredity added to the kind which they share with the animals. It is the social inheritance of which the animals show only a trace, if they show any at all. And by its means we of to-day are the heirs of the most of what we live by—our mother tongue, and the ideas at the back of its many thousand words, and its great literature. We of to-day add to this, but in a small way compared with the size and shape of what has come down to us from the past. And so it is with the customs that enter into house and home and family life; into trade; into the making of paper, books, and libraries; into schools and education; into musical instruments and concerts; into physiology and medicine and hospitals; into art, morals and religion. We of to-day build on foundations laid long ago, and add to or subtract from the abundance which was transmitted to us from earlier years of our own and every century before. Democracy is not of the making by men of to-day, nor is the experimental method in science; nor are universities and hospitals and theatres the works of the hands of us living men. We owe all these and more to men of an earlier time who passed these achievements on to us.

This manner of transmission and accumulation from generation to generation differs from that of biological inheritance in several weighty respects. It supplements mightily our animal mode of inheritance, and in a manner better befitting a life that is both creative and free.

For by social heredity what a person acquires, during his own lifetime, by his own or external powers is saved, and bestowed on later generations. By biological heredity alone these acquisitions would have been lost.

Mendel, at work in the garden of the Augustinian Monastery at Brno in Czechoslovakia—a visit to it more impressive than to many a shrine—observing his peas and pears, reasoned about what he saw and bequeathed to others a new insight which has changed the beliefs of multitudes the world over.

And its effect will continue as long as science lasts. Mendel did not inherit this insight of his; he inherited the power to attain it; and his attainment, achieved not by chromosomes and genes alone, but by inherited ways of tradition, became a possession of all.

Social heredity befits the ways of free men, in contrast to our animal heredity. For we are free to accept or reject, to extend or restrict what comes to us by social transmission. Thus has mankind rejected the ancient heritage of blood-vengeance and slavery. And men are painfully labouring against ancient political tradition aiming to make government more concerned with the welfare of every man. Social heredity leaves us free to accept or reject the offerings of a Mendel or Darwin, a Lincoln, or Wilson. It becomes a part of us; but only as we *make* it a part of ourselves. It is laid before us as is a treaty before a sovereign power, and we put to it, or refuse, our hand and seal. The animal has his chromosomes with their genes, and by them is in the hand of fate. We likewise have our chromosomes with their genes and begin life under their dictates. But besides this we are heirs of an abounding other wealth, the accumulated wealth which leaves us our liberty, and helps us to achieve still other liberties.

And as a closing comment; our social inheritance—unlike the bequest by our chromosomes which goes only to those in the strict lines of family descent—scatters its gifts like a sower, unniggardly, to an entire people, to a civilization of many peoples. Without it we should have no civilization.

III

Men and the animals differ greatly in the character of their environments, and in their relation to their environments.

Mankind, actually or potentially, has a physical environment immensely larger than that of the highest animals; and man controls that environment and makes it serve him in ways without parallel in the life of animals.

But with regard to their social environment there is no less great contrast between men and animals. Many of these creatures that are not men have their social life—the bees and ants, the birds, and the many mammals that live in small or large communities, within each of which there is some manner of common control of its members. With the animals, their communal life to-day, in the wilds scarcely touched by man, is probably almost precisely what it was in the distant past, stationary then as now.

But men, beginning with manners and a conscious life perhaps not far from those of the higher apes, showed a power to change the common life in many ways, as becomes creatures destined for liberty and new tasks.

Thus the community of the French to-day, for all its historic continuity, is unlike what it was before their Revolution; and still more unlike that of the Swedes, or Britons, or Chinese; not to speak of the tribal communities of Africa or Australia.

Besides the steady pressure of instinct and of their physical surroundings, these peoples are pressed into diverse shapes and move in diverse directions of effort because of being possessed by somewhat different affections and ideas, and goals. A human community can intentionally labour to preserve its own institution and ideals, or re-shape them, or cast some of them aside, as have the Russians of our day.

We observe no like power in animal communities to depart from their past.

We have still another kind of environment, the world of ideas and knowledge; of sentiments and guiding rules of action, of conscious right and wrong, of cast of will, of ideals that both shame and spur us on. This, in varying measure of breadth, depth and height, envelopes us and marks us as men, not beasts.

These mental surroundings vary with the eras of mankind, from cave man to farmer, to dweller in town with goods, good and bad; they differ among peoples of our own era, between Occident and Orient, between Canadians, Costa Ricans and Icelanders. Primitive love songs and religion reveal that even savages possess such a habitat of the human mind.

This dwelling-place of the mind is at once the most tenuous and the most energetic of humanity's surroundings. Thin air is coarse when fingered after it; its presence will not directly deflect the pointer of the most sensitive laboratory instruments. And yet its effects on the mind of a person, on a nation, is massive, compelling. It works on the comprehension, the affections, and the will; and plays its great part where a man stays loyal, as when the United States holds to her most humane institutions; or, when in contrast, Germany allowed Hitler and his dazzling design to take possession of its collective will and conscience. He and his crew had first of all to turn upside down and change left into right in the sphere of the German mind before he could lead the singing and be-bannered people into the abyss.

The environment of man is in part that of the animals, and then by his power he changes his physical environment according to his will. And then to this great novelty he adds another fashioned entirely out of the substance of the mind. He enspheres himself in an invisible world of ideas.

IV

And further, *of the struggle for existence*, which as we all know, is a common feature in men and animals.

The existence for which men come to struggle is not alone a living body, but a living body and mind peculiarly robust and furnished, ready to receive and entertain much that is new. Men who have advanced in human ways prepare for themselves novel means of sustenance, shelter and defence, and new liberties for enjoyment or for adventure. They create thousands of diverse employments and services—of baker, plumber, truckman; of actor and opera singer; of doctor and lawyer, and so on and on. Each of them has its part in re-making, for better or worse, the minds and bodies of those who fit themselves to these occupations, and of those who receive the services from them. The house painter and the naval captain struggle for and attain unlike kinds of existence, as do the jockey and the poet. Neither extreme would exchange places with the other. The man with his screw-driver and monkey wrench in the assembly line has his own satisfaction in that he is not the boss with his responsibilities and perhaps his obloquy. And when there is organized discontent, it indicates more than man's inhumanity to man; it indicates also a readiness for an adventure in new forms of collective action, toward a better existence than has yet been known. Men struggle not only for existence, but for an existence nearer to the good life.

There are varieties of human life, ready and waiting, almost regardless of occupation. In Berkeley one day there came to our house the strangest chimney-sweep—somehow clean as a whistle when the work began, and apparently no whit less clean when it ended. As he was leaving we fell into talk; he was found to be a Norwegian well versed in his country's literature, and personally acquainted with some of its living authors. More, he had his own cabin in the Sierra of California, where each year he spent the summer. He had been destined, of course, for the sea, but hated it, and to his family's amazement and chagrin he had chosen his present work which, he declared, he loved for the freedom it gave him. For he was his own master and could choose the hours and seasons of his work. Here was a quiet, nameless master of himself and much else in the world, creating for himself the kind of existence he desired. The life he chose to live with content is but a single instance of the countless varieties of life which men seek and find. In and around this work for a livelihood some find their way to their own kind of good life by friendship or writing or music, or by lending a hand to a children's hospital or to some social, political, or religious activity. The human struggle for existence thus has the diversity of substance in its means and ends that join in marking us as men.

So as we have seen, we differ from the animals not only with respect to the struggle for existence, but also in our manifold inheritance and in our limitless environment.

All told, there is little excuse for merely bemoaning the lot of man. We live a life of power and dignity and open ways ahead.

THE EMINENCE OF MAN

I

The belittling of men by many was set forth in the opening chapter of this writing. Science upon science, it is held, declares man to be less than a step-child in the immensity of the world; that he is a product of blind forces, and, throughout his brief life, powerless and helpless amid these blind forces.

A reply to such an account of man has been offered in the preceding chapters, and called *man's* reply. For in it his own behaviour and achievements have in the main been allowed to speak for themselves. The answer is thus concrete, without subtlety, or dogmatic denial as from a seat of authority. Nor has there been a rejection of any of the observed facts well established in any of the sciences—including anthropology, brain physiology, genetics, and all the rest. Instead facts upon facts neglected by these sciences have here been assembled; and from the more inclusive evidence, both physical and mental, have issued conclusions the direct opposite of the conclusions that man is nothing but. The larger picture should reveal more clearly the true stature of man. And in this picture there appears less of man's weakness, than of his strength; less of his subjection, than of his mastery; less of his lowly position and more of his eminence. It will now be well to bring together into clear view something of the range and quality of this strength and mastery, this eminence, which have already been before us but separate, and perhaps concealed by details; the woodland hidden by its trees.

II

And as we now view men in this clearer light, we see that they are not mere receivers through their sense organs of impressions from without, nor are they mere bundles of nerves and muscles reacting reflexively to external stimulation. Men, it is true, do receive certain stimulations from without, and sensations of many kinds in us are the result; they receive other stimulations, and reflex muscular acts of ours are the result. But this is not all. In the full picture is the power of man to initiate trains of events that are of a character quite different from our rudimentary responses of senses and muscles and biological drives. The difference is somewhat like that between the Mission of Santa Barbara as it stands, ready for worship, and the adobe and dry grass, of which its walls were largely made.

It would be well, now, to recall what was said in earlier chapters about man's constructive power. Man initiates changes in the realm of the lifeless, of earth, air, and water. He brings his mind to bear on his own society, and gives it new customs, institutions, laws and aims; and he extends the range of co-operation.

In all these enlargements of what has already existed, men's minds played the leading part. Bell invented the telephone by knowledge and understanding, by desire and continuing purpose. Peary found the Pole by knowing beforehand what he wanted to find and how to recognize it, and by an undaunted will to achieve his purpose. And so it was with them all. The feet, hands, voice and neural substance were indispensable, as were tools and instruments and a multitude of physical aids; but all these were subservient. The mind was their master and gave them its command.

III

In company with man's power to discover, invent, and create surpassingly, there actually is in him what would seem properly to belong only in that topsy-turvydom where Iolanthe's lover is half mortal and half fairy. In truth stranger still, man is wholly natural and also three-fourths of him is not natural.

By their creative power men achieve a new relation to the world of nature. They stand in nature and also stand above it. Man turns upon his own nature and the nature around and makes of himself a freed man.

To believe this we need but to recall that he takes his natural environment and adds to it an unnatural environment; that he takes his natural inheritance and complements it with an artificial, a socially transmitted inheritance; and that he takes his natural struggle for existence and augments this with a score of unnatural and preferred forms of existence, and modes of struggling for these. The anthropologist carefully distinguishes between the natural stone and the human re-shapings of it; calling these no longer facts of nature pure and simple, but artifacts, products of man's contriving. And may we not profitably think likewise of men untouched by human art, and men transmuted by men into blacksmith, schoolmasters and revealers of hidden truth? Men are thus both artifacts and artificers.

Liberty has been won; but far more. Men in millions, after breaking their shackles, have set themselves sturdily to learn and do more valued things.

The zoologists, the biologists, with their attention on man's bodily organs and their functioning; on his evolution and development, and much more, will continue, and rightly continue to count man a part of nature. But we may rightly raise a finger in warning when they and others, including not a few psychologists, say he is nothing more. As well say then the unearthed mortar and pestle is nothing but a part of nature.

Nor need we be silenced when we are made aware by sound research of the impossibility of showing exactly where man begins and animal ends; where animal begins and plant ends; where life begins and lifeless chemical action ends. Vague borders between human and lower animal life, between life itself and lifeless existence, are no good reason for there not being a real and significant difference between air, oaks, tigers and Edisons.

And especially shall we judge man not wholly by his physical structure and functions, but no less by his mental life and what he makes of it and does with it.

In truth, when we watch the creative doings of men and the doings of chimpanzees and gorillas, is not one led to conclude that in his unnatural, his artistic, his scientific, his moral and religious activity, man is as far from the ape as the ape is from the frog? Judging him by his body alone, we may properly call man a primate; no less immersed in nature than the others of this order, for this satisfies a certain need in classification. But taking due account also of the mind and its role in creative achievements must we not acknowledge man's eminence, his notable pre-eminence above all else in the nature known on earth?

IV

And with man's creative power and strange conjunction in him of the natural and the superior-to-nature, *mind—already present in the higher animals—comes in man to a new place and power, and attains its freedom.* In the animal world the mind serves the body; it aids its survival and its procreation. In man this relation of the two comes more and more to be reversed. The mind becomes increasingly the master, and watches over the body as over an indispensable and faithful servant of purposes freely created by the mind itself.

Men, moreover, commonly recognize the rare value of the mind. They come to prize it not only as a tool or instrument against threats to existence from animal, human and other perils; but men come to value their minds for the mind's sake alone. For their is nothing that so appalls the civilized man as loss or impairment of this centre of himself. And with all our admiration of brute strength in renowned lifter, boxers and wrestlers, in a Hercules, an Atlas—yet the far greater glory goes to the strong who die or suffer agony for an idea, in a splendid devotion—Prometheus, Samson or Socrates. And in time few trouble themselves with the muscles of their peoples' heroes, but speak first and longest of their sagacity, their foresight, their steadfast faith, their readiness to die rather than betray the cause. Only between nations, where almost universally barbarism and anarchy still prevail, does brute force hold its ancient value in men's minds. And here, though men prize it, they do so with horror of it; and labour for a better mind between peoples. Along with unstarved and uncrippled bodies, a better mind between nations and within nations is longed for and slowly attained. Here is a part of a long-continuing revolution bent on holding every inch of gain in the care for the human body, and yet establishing more firmly than ever, above this solicitude the authority of the mind.

V

Finally to this account of man and his creative ability, of his unique relation to nature, and his power and freedom of mind, there must be added that he *comes more and more into a conscious relation to the entire universe enfolding him*. Commonly men acknowledge an unperceived power greater than themselves and the observed world about them. They find their familiar world incomplete, even with all its living men; its land, seas and sky. Men press on through this and through their early representations of the unseen on to the great faiths of China, and India, of Persia and Palestine from which Europe, the Americas and the ends of the earth have received such lavish gifts. Nor does it seem likely that this augmenting of what is real for man is on less solid foundations than is our mental augmenting of physical sunlight which in fact lack the qualities we experience as colours—yet we transmute this colourless physical activity into the splendour of the rainbow; of sunrise and sunset. Nor is it on less sure foundation than is man's unhesitating confidence that his fellow men are more than their bodies; and that their conduct issues in large part from ideas and decisions of mind.

For in part the fateful affirmation of a reality superior to men and their observable surroundings is prompted by the self-same impulse from which science springs—from disciplined curiosity, from desire to understand. And where science stops, declaring it can as yet go no farther, other men's minds take up the task and give a general answer which makes this world more intelligible to them. It gives them the something needed to account for the whole marvellous system which science is exploring with such great success. And to the plain man it seems more reasonable to ascribe this system to an intelligent purpose than to ascribe it to unintelligent and purposeless energies, or else to leave it unexplained, or without attempt at explanation.

But in this complement to the scientific report, men find a satisfaction of more than their curiosity, of their desire to find the cause of what they observe. Especially do they find a satisfaction of their inborn and inbred desire for membership in a company fully worthy of their admiration and fealty. And in that faith from which Christendom takes its name, God would have men freely join him in the greatest of enterprises, the creation of a community of persons, each intent on the good life for all; happy or distressed according to the rate of their advance toward this goal or their distance from it. In such a universe, human life has dignity. The humane aim is also a divine aim. Each person is offered a post of honour, and is answerable for what happens there.

Eddington has said that whatever else God may be, He is a great mathematician. This came, for him, from a study of the physical world. From a study of the human mind, could well come the thought that whatever else God may be, He is no specialist, but a person to the full, careful of creative power in far from perfect persons, careful of its free exercise in a vast variety of materials and for the most diverse of aims.

Man thus is eminent above all else of eminence in this world of our perceptions—not in his native physical strength, but in his power to attain understanding of this world, and in his cunning and majestic additions to it. He learns to appreciate its beauty, even its sublimity and yet learns to value still more the best that issues from his own mind and the minds of his fellow-men; and, further, hosts of men become confident that a highest reality of the same kind is the source and meaning of the universe verified by our senses. Men thus assured can stand upright even in the horror and humiliation they persist in bringing on themselves —to which ample heed will be given later. They cannot agree with those who believe that man is merely an animal, or merely a mechanism, or merely an inert particle driven hither and yon by the wind. With difficulty and yet rightly we still may look out on our kind somewhat as did Miranda in the *Tempest*; or, soberer, as the Chorus in the *Antigone*, with mounting reason for proclaiming that of all the many wonders of the world, none is so wonderful as man.

II

LARGE REQUISITES FOR EXCELLENCE

A GEOGRAPHY OF TALENT

ALTHOUGH the ability to create is evident among peoples everywhere, from frozen north to frozen south, productivity is by no means evident in like measure throughout the world. And few indeed are the matters that exceed in interest or practical importance this contrast in effective talent. Is the distribution as though by chance alone, or does there appear to be anything orderly, anything that regularly accompanies the variations of this notable power, and might help toward its explanation? Is the contrast between peoples connected in any degree with soil or climate? or with difference of race? or of combativeness? or social stability? An intent though rapid look at such candidates for our acceptance will not be labour lost; particularly if the reader takes what here is offered for a starting point for his own fertile thought.

I

First then of soil and climate. Is man's productivity of mind, tongue and hand determined by richness or poverty of land, and water and by a moderate or extreme of temperature between arctic cold and torrid heat?

These externals count; they are congenial with constructive purpose or forbidding. But too large a role can be ascribed to them. Men are not always exceptionally creative wherever the physical surroundings seem most to favour it. In well-watered and temperate regions of the Americas, where now are the United States, Brazil, and Argentina, the aborigines, it is true, had their craftsmanship, their arts; their able warfare; but never —so far as we yet know—had they the opulence of accomplishment that marks similar or even less favoured regions of Europe and of Asia; such as marks Italy and Greece, Arabia, Palestine, Persia, India and China. Not from the Americas, nor from the whole continent of Africa, outside the valley of the Nile, came the varied and humane institutions of justice and education and government; came the literature and science, or the philosophy and religion which these other lands have bequeathed to all mankind.

II

Next, of race, of which there is to-day passionate assertion and denial. Let us as best we can detach ourselves from the outrageous dogma of Hitler and his criminals, and accept as fact that no race is pure, and also that we are still ignorant of the origin of races and of their fundamental likeness or difference of mind. And yet we cannot overlook the fact that both in our practice and in our thinking and customs, we distinguish four stocks of mankind—the Blacks, the Browns, Yellows, and Whites. And these we may continue to call races. And, out of two of these—the Mongoloids and the Caucasians—have come the most creative peoples of the ancient and the modern world.

The White race and the Yellow race above all others are creators of urban life, of civil life, and all that is meant by civilization.

Scientists are far from agreed as to the *explanations* of this strange fact. But this should cast no doubt on the fact itself—that within two races there has appeared an amount and range of creative work that far exceeds what has been accomplished in the other races. These others are creative in remarkable ways, so that this ability exists throughout mankind, but in markedly unequal measure on opposite sides of a great racial division among men.

III

Life in a community, as will be explained later, is one of the indispensables of all but the rudiments of creative work.

But the community need not be immense in order to bring forth what deserves renown. Denmark, Czechoslovakia, the Swiss, leave us in no doubt of this. Nor need the creative community be small, as is shown of old by Egypt, Rome and China; and later by Germany in her prime, the British Empire and the United States. Yet size is not wholly without significance. A family, clan, or tribe, if its community does not extend beyond this narrow limit, is too small to offer to talent all that is required.

But the extent of a community is not to be confused with its political boundaries. The Scandinavian countries are one in much that weighs in our present scale. And small states elsewhere, as in ancient Greece, and in the League of the Hanseatic towns, or in the Italy of Dante's time—each member, in many ways not political, felt itself a member of a fellowship far beyond its own small self; and in creative worth could stand head-up beside empires. The small German States, in the days before Prussia and Frederick and Bismarck had done their sorry work, made treasure for the world. England made what was of deathless worth while she was mistress of but a part of one small isle.

This is no condemnation of continent-wide communities, but only of the idea that immensity does of itself give birth to the concerted abilities we are here considering. The community enlarged by ties across national boundaries—as between Britain and the United States, and between the Scandinavian countries—makes it clear that the benefits of immensity can be won without outward shift of a national boundary.

IV

The highly talented peoples—in general those of the Caucasian and the Mongoloid races as said earlier—have also been peoples intent on war. For the ancient literature of both the Jews and the Chinese, who in our day have seemed pacific, is not without more than a breath of the Prussian spirit. And shall we then hold that here is the secret of talent's strange distribution over the face of the earth?—that warfare is, as eminent minds in our day have declared, the source of all the virtues, of all political skill, of the arts and sciences?

One may doubt the truth of this since many a people not eminent in the arts of peace, in creative work, were fierce warriors —the Tartars, the several earlier peoples of the Americas, in Mexico especially, and among the Redskins of the North; the Turks and, as Xenophon's Ten Thousand knew, the Armenians of an earlier day. If war were of itself creative beyond all else, then the Balkans would have been a centre of advancing civilization in modern Europe.

Indeed, history and the lengthening story of the times before history, these suggest that warfare indulged in with drunkard incontinence, may well have been a chief cause of the very lack of high creativeness in some of the races of mankind that actually have in many respects rare natural endowment. For the Redskins, the Browns and the Blacks have marvels of native ability that has never come fully into its own. None of them has produced such communities as alone can afford some of the indispensables for still further creativity, soon to be considered.

Now, psychologists have not found in the several races any such contrast in the native intelligence as would account for their contrast in advance into civilization. And if differences in the native power to know, to understand, are insufficient to account for these results, is there any other feature in endowment to which we may look? Yes, for it is not impossible that in the insufficiently explored realm of the emotions and the impulses something of what we seek may be found; and the contrast in ability to create suitable communities may be due in no small measure to an excessive play of those emotions and impulses—anger, fear, distrust, hatred, and a thirst for vengeance—which divide men and keep them in small groups.

The readiness for comradeship and fellow-action, native to all men, has here remained ill-developed; and indeed there has been an inordinate cultural encouragement of the opposing, the divisive passions by giving these a pre-eminent sanction in morals and religion, and by strengthening them into such institutions as blood-vengeance, and into a life-long pre-occupation with inter-tribal war.

Here the small communities have remained small, and psychically alien to one another, with resultant loss of all those benefits which come only by fairly wide co-operation, and by pooling all the abilities of a large population.

The Caucasians and the Mongoloids, who seem the most quarrelsome and ferocious of all mankind, with their devastating armaments, have, however, attained this eminence by their further ability to bring a large and then a larger population into a peaceable domestic life of co-operation and practical unity. From such ability to temper warfare with wide fellowship came nations, terribly destructive, but also creative beyond all others, bringing men to the beginnings of an extended civil life. These two great races are now being tested as never before to discover whether their ability to understand and co-operate can grapple successfully with their pugnacity, and extend still further communal ties and thus save from an unparalleled ruin their hard-won gain of centuries.

But the stability here required is not rigidity, not stagnation. The quartz crystal is not its symbol, nor is the Dead Sea. The needed stability will involve change, incessant change, but with the constancy, the regularity, the integrity of variation found in a young fir, or, better, in a youth headed for uncommon skill and wisdom. The steady company of men will have a constant, though distant goal for its movement and a fluid choice of the means and ways to the goal. It will be intolerant of fixity in what has been socially achieved, eager for what is better; intolerant also of those who are ready to destroy every good we have to-day to have a new world to-morrow.

Thus in every people on our globe, even in the most backward, is there the ability to create what until then did not exist—tools and ornament, songs, and law, and prayers to an unseen power. But not everywhere has this ability come to an equal profusion and excellence of result. And one can hardly be satisfied with those who would account for this disparity by differences in the physical surroundings of men—climate, soil and more. And so we have turned with hope to forces within man, forces native and acquired, hardly more than introduced in the present chapter, but which will in pages to follow be examined as they repeatedly appear before us.

INDISPENSABLES FOR CREATIVE POWER

I

Necessity alone is not the Mother of all our inventions. Has it not long been *necessary* that we have a cure for domestic crime and for war? Or have those great inventions for science, the telescope, microscope and radio, issued from a compelling need for them? Nor do talent and a persevering will suffice. Leonardo had both of these for human flight; and flight did not come for centuries later, with the strange type of engine undreamt of by Leonardo.

What, then, are some of the requirements for achievement here, beside strength of body and mind and the things which life and strength themselves demand?

With bare hands men can do much, but not the wonders of any civilization, such as that represented by the ruins of Egypt and Yucatan, or by the living cities of Peking and in contrast, New York. For, to create and maintain a civilization, men need tools, instruments. One invention or discovery must come and show the way to another; stone implements before those of copper and iron. In Honolulu one may see the wooden forerunners of the sextant, for use in coming across wide stretches of the Pacific. On top of the wall of Peking are old bronze astronomical instruments, of the best design and workmanship possible until the telescope, spectroscope and photography came into the making of to-day's astronomy.

A host of engines powered by hand or foot, by dead-weight, by the flow of water, by the strength of ox or ass, incited men to add to these many another engine, with the power of steam, and later of gas, then electricity and to-morrow the energy within the atom. The aeroplane had to wait for the gas engine; the telephone, radio, radar and imaginably more could not be created until men had made generators and could harness electric power. Medicine could not become what now it is without microscope, stethoscope and microtome; without galvanometer and cardiograph, to say nothing of all that physiology and psychology have to offer.

Thus in every industry, in every enterprise of communication or transport, in every weather-station, laboratory or hospital of to-day, are tools, instruments, machines which have issued from the mind and then given indispensable aid to the further work of creative power. From man with flint-tipped spear to man in

Cairo sending his voice to San Francisco, creativity in many an instance has had to stand stock-still until instruments had been contrived to help him on his way.

II

Creative power, moreover, would never have come into its own, indeed would never have created most of the instruments just indicated had men not created language which is the great means to still greater means and ends, to be noticed later.

For without language there would never have come into being advanced science and many of the great arts and all other of man's highest achievements. Without the astronomy before Galileo's day there would have been no call for such use of his optic glass by the Tuscan artist; nor would there have been brought into being the telescope on Palomar with its glass more than sixteen feet across. Astronomers had to speak to meteorologist, engineer, technicians in glass, and many others, to make this mighty tool of the eye and mind. And the astronomer had to communicate with astronomers around the world—and also through long nights and years with himself—to know the instrument's right use. Language, spoken, written, printed, is in its value far beyond even hand or eye—it is the greatest instrument for making all but the most primitive instruments of creative will. It makes possible also some indispensables of productive will, indispensables which should next be brought to mind.

III

For all important creativity, no one person is enough; many, often myriads, have done their part. What could your genius in engineering have done at Panama, in the Tennessee Valley, or on the Columbia River, if he and other men by thousands had not worked together—men who had the general purpose uniting with men who could work out its details; men who could persuade farmers and shop keepers and officers of government, and in the end win the nation's support, and have the work begin. One need not trace out the complexity of co-operation which these set afoot until the immense work was ready for use. No wonder-work of old mythology could equal one of these achievements of modern men at work together—from genius down to the unskilled labourer with shovel in hand or lifting a bag of cement.

But what of the artist at work, not with concrete and steel, but with his own mind only, and doing what he can do in his own home, with help in little more than his meals, or in recording what he has inwardly brought to being—Beethoven, deaf, composing symphonies he was never to hear; or blind Milton, his epic born within him, and he dictating it to others?

Indeed is not the best of art, then, given to genius by an inner inspiration, the mind better if alone and protected by triple bronze against the intrusion of other minds?

It is never so; this idea is a delusion of individualists. Beethoven, before his deafness, had made his own whatever he most prized of Europe's music; had heard his compositions played and knew them to be acclaimed in the capitals of his art world. By these were his gifts nurtured; they encouraged him, worked with him as he worked.

And Milton had all Christendom at his side, working with him. He studied, travelled, and was highly favoured. He shared its learning, its taste, its political and moral aims; its faith encompassed all he wrote. Thus even in his blindness his powers were drawing from the work of others; they were joining with his genius; he and they co-operated to make true of him Wordsworth's great sonnet. In ways like these do not only geniuses, but far lesser men as well, bring their full talent to the world's treasury. The whole and each contribution to it comes of co-operation. Every creator has worked with others to acquire language, skill, knowledge; he and others working with him bring him to wider interest and appreciation, and open before him a larger opportunity than would be his by his own solitary power. Without this co-operation, the mind never comes to flower and fruit.

IV

Further gain must be joined with gain, through years, through centuries, for great achievement. Even co-operation, necessary as it is, comes to no generous result if it breaks fully from all that precedes it, and remains apart from the stream of later creative work. There must be continuity, gains amassed in the long course of time.

To illustrate this we may take the ocean liner of to-day, which in the wonder of it tops anything told by Sindbad the Sailor. It is the product of a great and unbroken tradition of gradual changes through centuries, indeed millenniums of venturesome trials—changes in the shape and size of hull, from that of the crude raft, coracle and canoe, to the oared galley of the Mediterranean, the Viking vessels that could brave the North Sea and the Atlantic, to the vessels of the fleet of Columbus; on to the Great Eastern and the most recent Atlantic liner.

And the means of *moving* this ever-enlarging hull and its burden of men and wares had a like growth—from hand paddle to oar and oar-lock, to a line of oars, to tier upon tier of oars; from small single sail to many large sails, rigged more and more adroitly, more completely to the magnificence of canvas from stem to stern and up to the main topgallant sail. And then added to sail, came steam with boiler added to boiler, on to a battery of engines without steam. And along with all these came the growth of much else, including the use of charts, compass, and of the instruments for knowing where the ship is by sighting the sun or other heavenly bodies. Little by little all this was done by a marvel of conservation of past gains together with bold addition of what had never been so used before. Little wonder that, for the men who live and labour, and learn confidence in a ship, is she given an endearing name, and her loss at sea is mourned as the death of a friend.

The Temple of Athena, in the city of her name, was no product of its own time alone, but by an accumulation and selection of features issuing from centuries of effort in Greece and elsewhere in the eastern Mediterranean. The effort was in the arts and sculpture needed for the Parthenon, and was continuous, in that the later artists had at hand the fruits of their predecessors, studied them, respected them, and at once imitated and freely modified what had been handed down.

v

Yet it hardly need be added that it is possible to over-do our homage of the past. To add excellence to excellence requires a nice weighing of honouring and independence in due proportion. The Chinese, so inventive, so adventurous in many ways, have probably not until recently tempered sufficiently their reverence for the past with this spirit of adventure.

The Mayas of to-day, on the other hand, illustrate probably the result of the almost complete disruption of its tradition. For we have been told that they are of the same stock, with the same biological endowment of those Mayas from whom came marvels of monumental buildings of bold and refined architecture and with carved records and calendar through long reaches of time. Of these, the present Mayas dwelling there, can give no satisfactory account. Even the tradition of them has perished, so great was their social disintegration.

Each social treasure of modern or ancient times has come into being by means of common and rare instruments, and by a gradual summation of lesser benefactions usually in the course of centuries. And for the crowning outcome men have worked with other men near and far, with men famous or forgotten, of to-day, yesterday and the distant past. The present thus comes into a rich inheritance and may bequeath it multiplied to the men of to-morrow.

THE ENCOMPASSING COMMUNITY

The native powers of the person, whether they be those of exceptional talent or of the plain mind, are shaped and directed largely by the nation and the civilization in which he is reared and prepared for his labour. This is true of Browning, of Darwin, of Einstein. Even the rebels like Marx and his follower Lenin show this influence in their revolt. The Man is not made, wholly, soul and body, by his community, but this communal influence is so nearly fateful for the product of his talent that we must look attentively at it.

I

The strong desires of a people are a large part of this invisible pressure on the worker's will. What are the directions in which a people's affections most strongly turn, and in which its thought runs, day and night? What are the directions in which any progress brings rejoicing, and in which regression means woe? Answer this, and there is found the magnetic point to which the people's will most readily turns, and if swerved away, returns.

But the compass and the pole are no suitable symbols of a people's strong desires. For these may be many, as with the Greeks, whose range of notable achievements include sculpture and architecture, written history and drama, science and philosophy. And the Jews have shown themselves master workmen in music and letters, in science and philosophy, in commerce, and, above all else, as revealers of moral and religious truth. The French, the Germans, and the English have each a wondrous variety of interest and achievement. One is led, in consequence, to regard a people's mind as possessed of many talents whose fields are not so specialized by nature as some have believed, but are capable of any one of most varied results, depending much on the opportunities to acquire skill, or on the appreciation, the understanding, the encouraging interest waiting ready for the young.

The desires or interest shared affects the use made of what is transmitted from the past; deciding what from the heritage shall be cherished, and what shall be thrown aside. These ruling desires largely shape also the current co-operation; for heart goes into work whose product is widely prized. And where the chief satisfaction is in successful warfare, as once in Sparta, in Prussia and its Germany and in the France of various centuries, there the best talent presses forward to invent for war and do in war what never had yet been done. If, on the contrary, there is a collective interest first of all, for music, painting, sculpture, and monumental architecture, as it was in Italy of the Renaissance, talent, genius then comes forth eager for origination in the favoured field.

The United States has many a desire important for the nation's will, but two are eminent, the one, political, the other, economic. And in these—beyond all else—have we laboured with a will and with collective and individual genius.

Russia, by her revolution, has likewise put economics and politics above all else, with science and art their ministers. But in general these two commanding interests are more intense and exclusive with them than with us. For in the United States the spirit of liberty and the spirit of Christianity restrain, even though they fail to master our love of politics and our love of what money can buy. And in both countries the desire for national power and place in the society of nations is reaching an ominous intensity.

Such are but hints of what, if fully told, would be the psychic climate of a people, and which deeply influences its craftsmanship, its art, its moral life, and the force and quality of its ideas.

II

Thus far the community's part in productive labour may seem that of the bracing salt sea for the swimmer; it invigorates him, bears him up, offers resistance and fulcrum for his propelling strength. But its part in the final product, often is more than this. The community takes a more important hand in shaping the very product itself, becomes in fact a fellow-artist, inventor or craftsman. Individuals must have made the products, but not working as detached individuals. The work grew by concerted accretions, the unpremeditated variations of which were spontaneously accepted as slightly better fulfilling the collective purpose, and were thereafter repeated in the common life and carried farther still. Generation after generation improved and enlarged the creative work, as in those terraces, cultivated, watered, line above line, covering whole mountainsides in the Ifugao country of the Philippines. The individuals shared in a public purpose which stirred to invention and daring and continued labour almost beyond belief. The continuity of all such labours of a community can overcome the impetuosity or sloth of private persons, others coming in to fill the gaps made by sickness or death—decade after decade, often century after century. The common purpose of men in a common life cannot here be omitted in explaining those products we admire.

III

But the creative will of the community—extended out into a nation, or even to the peoples of a common civilization—is no less present in those products where historic personal names emerge in the people's creative work, and are honoured as founders, or givers of great gifts. This probably is true of much of those common obligations, or laws ascribed to Moses, the Ten Commandments, the Five Books of the Law. It is clearly true of the Common Law of the English-speaking lands, though individuals have won renown in dealing with it—Blackstone and many more. And similarly of much of International Law with which the name of Grotius is inseparably associated. A large part of all such law is the collective and prevailing judgment of men living a life in common, on the rights and wrongs of their important dealings with one another. No separate individual, no number of separate individuals has thought out this part of law. The community as a whole, through centuries of clash and settlement, has brought it forth.

To these examples should be added others—the established moral code of a people, the manner of its government, the democratic way of government, each great religion. A single shrine of a people, such as Canterbury Cathedral, may both illustrate and symbolize this communal participation in a creative work whose every stone has been hewn and placed by individual men. But these hands and the personal will they served, were commanded by the authority of a people whose common life had deepened and widened through centuries—a people that itself was enlivened profoundly all the while by a great faith they shared with men far and wide. The Cathedral speaks of all this and of much more that could never be expressed in words—of St. Augustine, of Anselm, of Becket; of tragedy and triumph, of fidelity and aspiration, in which the men of any particular time held fellowship with the noblest in themselves, in those of an earlier epoch, and with those still to come. The Cathedral represents what seemed to them the greatest and best in the common life; and this reach of the spirit for what is greatest and best has through ages been directing the minds and hands of men everywhere.

And so it is—changing the words as befits the particular—with all new results which a people enduringly holds dear. The man does what no other man could match precisely; his own individuality looks out from it. But unmistakably he could never have fashioned his unique product unless his people, his community, had entered into him and worked with and through him.

IV

The community here in mind evidently will include those of a person's face-to-face acquaintance in his own town and countryside. But it also extends to those far off, never seen in the flesh, but with whom he feels he belongs and who have contrived to make him theirs. A nation, a commonwealth of nations, is such a company, in which the mutual ties of mind call forth the embracing 'we' and 'our'. It is in some measure a communion not entirely of the saints. And even in so faulty a communion as the nation, the ties of fellowship extend into the distant past and the distant future. But not a few Americans have lived their best years in England or France or China and gradually have found themselves bound in spirit in an enlarged fellowship. Others are hardly willing to call any one deeply theirs; and their community, though they know the world, is perhaps less than a parish. Yet they have received much from many, and many lands and eras unthanked may work in them, and help inform their product with rare knowledge and grace.

There are those who say of a man's community that it is only his jail, from which he must escape to become an individual.

Especially in America is this bit of imagination held for wisdom. It is the height of unrealism—along with that opposite idea that a man is made by his society from top to toe. The present account of the matrix of talent, when joined with chapters to follow, will, it is hoped, present a juster view; leaving us no less responsive than before to the mood: 'Let us now praise famous men, and our Fathers that begat us'; and be as ready with an added strophe, in praise of famous communities without which these men and our fathers would not have become worthy of renown.

A HERMIT OF THE SIERRA

I

There came to my study at the University years ago, a man who gave an unusual and moving account of himself in the unhurried visit. His life had been largely spent alone, far from men, in the California Sierra, his solitude broken only at long intervals by his descent to some outpost for his few wants.

And through the years his mind had been busied, above all else, in arriving at an answer to questions about the world around him; not about distant human affairs, nor the near-by animals and plants, and all their enigmas for us; but concerning lifeless nature—light and darkness, sound and silence, heat and cold, and more. And he had come to what was for him a complete scientific understanding of them all. He seemed ignorant or else wholly negligent of what others had done and were doing in this realm, and believed he had of himself by his own naked observation and thought, a knowledge of the full truth about these things.

And now at last he had come to a seat of scientific research where, he had been confident, his discoveries would be understood and welcomed. But instead, the physicists whom he had just visited, he told me, had heard coldly, without comprehension. (And so, as is the wont in such matters, to be rid of him, they had referred him to a psychologist.) He was amazed, benumbed. 'Why are these men,' he said in substance, 'so closed of mind, so unready to see that I have *found*, and was

LARGE REQUISITES FOR EXCELLENCE

now offering them what they have for so long been seeking!'

And as he then more definitely told me of his findings, I listened in dismayed sympathy. For it was as though there had been misplaced into our own era some one, half scientist, half seer, of an earliest period of Greek reflection on these matters, of a time, perhaps, before Thales. For he seemed a man of unusual gifts, not diseased in mind, one that—if he had lived in those olden days of the Eastern Mediterranean—might well have left us an imperishable name.

Why, then, was he brushed aside by the physicists? Was it because they lacked patience, or could not recognize truth when it came to them? I feel sure this was not so. The man did not have the truth; they perceived this, and for them he was but one more crank, and cumbered the ground.

II

In this man, if I mistake not, was ability, perhaps rare ability, its work directed with no mean aim. But this endowment of his had been applied fruitlessly, the labour lost. How could this be?

The failure may seem the more puzzling, for the hermit had acquired many of the indispensables set down in the preceding chapters, and others not named there at all. That his ability was intellectual, was evinced by the problem he had set himself to solve; no half-wit would have done this. Further, he had acquired a fair mastery of the first necessary instrument for intellectual production, namely, a rich language, English, which showed that he had spent some of his early years with men of a civilized culture, with its special interests and ideas. And still further, he had attained an unusual independence, a self-reliance, so important for originality in production. His separation from men was not that of a lost child, or an abandoned babe. He could freely return to the community of men when he chose; and had freely done so, repeatedly before he came on his strange visit to the University. And in his earlier life he probably had heard or read enough of physics to acquaint himself with at least the surface of some of its affirmations.

To many a person of our day all this would seem the very perfection of readiness for creative work in the field of his lively interest and of his steadfast purpose. But in fact his complete self-confidence was his undoing.

For, first of all, he had entered on an enterprise without scientific instruments and probably without the knowledge to use them profitably if he had taken them to his mountains. He was self-confident, and may have despised them then, believing that he could arrive at what he sought by his own unaided, eyes, ears and mind. His first lack, then, was that of some of the necessary tools for his work at its present state of development. The ancient Greek scientists got along without brass instruments, they lived before the period of laboratory experiment.

His second lack was that he had not come into his full heritage of knowledge already acquired for his enterprise and which was awaiting him. He either was ignorant of most of this, or else cast it aside, as he had the needed laboratory instruments.

Finally, he had not entered into the indescribably broad and complicated mind-to-mind co-operation with scientists in his own time, near and distant, by close association, meetings and published writings, without which no work of note is done to-day, such as he had undertaken and believed he had ended with success. He certainly had not sought and received the criticism, the appreciative advice of those at hand; and the examples, the suggested cautions from the current publications of men in foreign lands. He had not sought this help nor felt the need of it. He had failed to seek and receive the co-operation necessary to turn the tragedy of his failure into distinguished success.

One is reminded of the report—for us an allegory—by the mystic Swedenborg, of an angel who believed he could cut himself off from the other angels and live well alone. Instead, when he attempted it, he was as a babe, and could neither walk nor talk.

The Hermit of the Sierra illustrates what occurs when in science to-day one makes an attempt like this. Its meaning, however, is wider than the particulars of his case. It speaks of what is indispensable in all notable production, not only throughout science, but in technology, in civic enterprise, in the healing arts, in the fine arts, and in the finest of all arts, that of living as men would have themselves live, and of participating in the creation of such a life.

III

FROM APPRENTICESHIP TO MASTERY

PLOWING AND SEEDTIME

I

THE effect on the person of his early human surroundings may be concretely illustrated. Thus a friend and former student of mine—whose home was in Hawaii—she herself a white woman, gave me a careful report of a well-known acquaintance of hers, a young woman, Japanese by birth, whose parents had tried to drown her at birth. A married couple, on whose plantation the attempt was made, discovered the infant, brought it to their home, and from then on cared for her quite as though she were their own daughter. Her associates were whites only, and she was educated with and by whites.

The result was, that while in physical features and perhaps also in a slight peculiarity of gait she was Japanese, yet she had no desire to be with Japanese, and in speech, thought, and conduct she was in no respect different from other well-bred, well-educated white women of the Islands.

And even where the child's transfer to an alien race is somewhat later than that of the infant in Hawaii, the result is no less astonishing. To speak briefly of what the writer has re-counted in some detail elsewhere, some white children in early days in America were captured by Indians, grew up with their captors to full maturity, and were accepted fully as members of the tribe. And when found by Whites the persons had become one in mind with those of Indian birth—in language and in minor ways of behaviour, of course, but no less in ideas, beliefs, purposes and loyalties.

The human beings with whom the child lives and with whom he is nurtured lay hold on the child's powers and set them to work according to the ways of body and mind—the customs, institutions, the convictions and ideals; that is, the 'culture' of these fosterers of the child.

II

But from now on we may consider only the child who has undergone no dislocation, but is reared by his own parents and among his own race and culture.

In the home the normal child begins his apprenticeship in the great and unspecialized art of quitting himself like a man. And in this humane instruction the mother is by nature and much else, and often for life, foremost. But when it comes to the lad's choice of his life-work, the father's deepest interest may weigh heavily even if not decisively.

Of moment, often, is a recognition and encouragement of the child's ability. Lincoln received a saving touch of this sympathetic spur from his step-mother, beginning long after his first three years when, as has been asserted by some in our day, the child's whole future is written down and the book closed. In Lincoln's case, this discerning woman, seeing the boy's eagerness for reading, let the boy read and read and also get what schooling was within reach. Thus a door was opened toward mastery of that instrument, spoken and written English, without which even such a spirit as his could hardly have led his people through their deadly peril.

Or, for an instance nearer the present time, and of polar contrast to that of Lincoln, William James began life in a home suffused and enveloped with the best in culture and spirit. In it with the years were, among others, the brother, Henry, younger than William by a year; a sister, Alice, to whom William, when away, wrote intimately and with affectionate delight; and the mother and father, both of them sympathetic and unworldly. The father, for whom religion and speculation were the head and heart of all he thought and did, was the opposite of a tyrant in the family. And yet all the while, such was his character, he towered there massively.

In the home were books and books; there were famous friends and visitors; Emerson and Carlyle were familiar spirits; and near by was an eminent seat of learning. Thus from childhood excellent things, overflowing, were within reach of a mind exceptionally inquisitive and outreaching.

The sympathetic understanding between father and son, for all their difference, was full and enduring. And in the many years when William was groping for his work, the father, while having his own judgment and choice in the matter, kept hands off. He wished and successfully sought to give the lad the widest opportunity and liberty for decision. Henry James, the elder, something of a seer and prophet, was without warmth for either literature or science for his sons. And yet he gladly gave to each of them freedom to explore these two subjects and finally adopt as his own choice, letters for Henry; and science—within an unorthodox breadth of philosophical horizon—for William; and this without rupture or chill on either side. It is hard to imagine a finer achievement in the family life.

This is no place to recount the various experiments and rejections by William in letters, painting, anatomy, physiology, before finding at last his place in psychology and philosophy.

The young William James, still in his own home, even while thousands of miles from it, illustrates our topic with a clearness hardly to be surpassed. This propitious household gave him understanding and affection and courage; it sharpened and enriched him; it set him free in a universe both known and mysterious; it helped him with his rare endowment, to become a wise seeker and discoverer of what many have come to believe in and to love.

There seems to be no one kind of home from which alone a child's talent can issue—provided opportunity is offered, not too late for acquaintance with the larger world of civilization. The least propitious was that of Lincoln, just recalled. The human spirit is of a vitality, striking its roots down through riven granite, and growing against icy wind. The rugged Scottish child in America, John Muir, survived and somehow thrived under a fanatical tyrant father; and in spite of it all, continued to the end a lover of both men and animals, and not only of forests and glaciers. Other men who produce richly, are from infancy lapped in comfort, affection and appreciation, as was Mendelssohn. A mystery is in this nurture of ability, even with all our growing knowledge. And to say that genius can survive the most untoward cradling, does not mean that rare ability is reckless of its whereabouts. To the contrary, some surroundings of childhood are markedly more propitious than others. Facts of many kinds have left undenied witness to this. Cases of a single kind must alone be mentioned.

The parsonage, perhaps because of the favourable genes there, but also because of the interest, both in religion and also in character, education, and in humane living, has long been an early proving ground for later achievement. The Brontës were fledged and fostered in a vicarage. And Visher found that in the United States a surprisingly large proportion of distinguished persons had clergymen as their fathers; indeed, that in proportion to the numbers of such fathers in our population, the clergy's homes brought forth twice as many notables as did the homes of all other professional men classed together, and four times as many as did the homes of business men. This, along with the usual austerity of such homes among us, is one more bit of frowning evidence added to much else against a current creed that all will be well with the world when every house has in it everything it can buy from the ten-storied department store.

Food, clothing, and a fire, enough for life and health, these must indeed be there. But beyond these, talent needs above all else its touch with human beings, living far from the beasts, and giving the child the beginning of his absorption of the life and culture and sentiments of his people. He needs to feel himself one with them, and ready to work with them; to understand what will fortify and enlarge them, and to augment this from his own inner resourceful will and spirit.

III

Already while in the home the child, the youth, has been reaching out beyond the home for his nutriment and rejoicing. Yet the home remains in him, even though it may have become hateful, a thing to be torn out of him. But even so, it need not compel him to its own direction. Instead, its wind toward the south-west, with sail well set, speeds him south-east, or, by tacking, dead north-east. Yet, often in due time, it heads him into its own quarter of the compass. So it was for Augustine, who, after years, returned into the way of his mother, Monica, and in it does a thousandfold more than even his home had shown him. And the poet Thompson, trying through the years to escape, is pursued and at last overtaken by the Hound of Heaven.

In the years when the home is most potent, other forces are being added to it, by lecturers and fellow scholars, by friendships, face to face with the young and the less young; friendships also through reading. And added to these is the whole wide range of in-coming observations of persons, and notable machinery; the natural world of birds and plants, and an animal or two even in a city. And some travel, in the United States at least, some travel is inevitable—by long walks, by automobile, train, ship or aeroplane; the very home itself on wheels.

IV

And let an instance of such diversity be Masaryk in his early years. His early life gives one vividly far more than would any lifeless list of forces that, beyond the home, shape the youth toward full creative power.

His father's occupation, that of coachman to a landed gentleman, did not for long, if ever, capture the lad's will. Nor was he captured by his apprenticeship to a locksmith. But importantly he learned to read, and in time to value an immense range of reading, as is testified by his library in the old palace on the heights looking down on Prague's patined domes, and its gleaming river richly bridged—there on the height, in view of all this beauty, was Masaryk's personal collection of thousands of books, not merely collected, but read, with passages marked and noted in his own hand—books in many languages, from many a people's literature. For he was bent on understanding peoples, nations; and he held a nation's literature to be a key for this understanding—as our own universities, including their psychologists, are belatedly being urged to believe.

And in Masaryk's preparation this copious reading was conjoined with study in school and university, and with teaching philosophy. He also, in the years before his culminating work, discussed important affairs from the platform and by writing. High in his training, too, was his membership in the Diet of the Dual Kingdom of Austria-Hungary, of which his homeland was then a part. He laboured with those who sought autonomy for his people. And later, in many lands, including Russia and the United States, he travelled, lived and worked untiringly. All the while he was preparing for his country a government by and for its people, rock-based on education, free discussion, patience, and religion.

Thus his quick intellect and sympathy and will are amply stored and disciplined for his final great achievement, now again suppressed from without.

This illustration from the field of statecraft, however, is not for the understanding of creative statecraft only. Changing what should be changed, it holds also for all preparation—in science, in the technical arts and in all that pours forth from the mind's horn of plenty.

TOWN AND COUNTRYSIDE

I

The work-place and its surroundings are of great moment for some workers, and of little for others. There are men so aflame with purpose, so stored within, and with such a task in mind, as to be at it wherever they are, whatever may be at hand —in plenty or in want; in freedom or in prison; in factory-town or by field and stream. In some the heart cries out for congenial externals; with others, nothing counts but the work, the work itself.

To be definite, your inventor of machines may be helpless without his work-bench and tools, perhaps his laboratory with electric power, lathes, materials, chemicals; perhaps a furnace or wind-tunnel or testing machinery tower-high; and he must live where such things can be erected, housed and manned.

The composer of music, however, would wither and die in such surroundings; yet he has his own aids. In an earlier day this might be a princely court, or a church with its organ, its skilled singers, and an appreciative audience. Would Bach in burgher Leipzig have wrought his great works without the aid of orchestra and organ and without his boys of the *Thomanerschule* to render many of them on festal days of church and city?

Letters, in contrast, is of all production the least querulous, the least demanding as to externals. Its devotees, given ink and paper, bring forth deathless things in all manner of circumstances—Paul, a prisoner in Rome; the seer John on his rocky isle; Bunyan in jail; Shakespeare, managing and acting in his theatre; Wordsworth by his lakes; Whitman in Brooklyn; Emerson and Hawthorne and Thoreau in Concord or not far away.

II

Later, in attempting an appraisal of the physical influences quite beyond the immediate place of the man's work, the city will have its due. But here and now let justice be done to meadow and stream, to forest and mountain, and to the mystery of sea and sky. Imagine the world bereft of all who ever loved and painted these marvels; bereft of all their paintings and of all memory of them!

And the same is true of writers who have looked with heart and spirit behind their eyes upon the outer miracles and revealed these to us. So that by the magic of Shakespeare we see the meadow painted with delight, and the morning sun flattering the mountain top with sovereign eye.

III

As a mere hint of what nature has said to some philosophers, Berkeley believed that every colour, every sound, every other sensation of ours that tells of cloud, flower, rock or waterfall is but a fragment of a divine language, is a syllable in the utterance by which God speaks to the minds of men. Nor will any one fail to recall Kant, whose depths of the spirit responded to two things above all else—to the heavens above, and to the moral law within.

And many of the great leaders of religion were immeasurably indebted to the impression of outer nature upon them, leaving them lonely, or befriended; intellectually disquieted, or exalted by mystic intercourse with the divine. The world over, on island and headland, on fertile plain or on desert, such men have received at least an intimation of life greater than their own; in storm-cloud, the lightning, and the crash of thunder, in wind and rain, in flower and tree. This is seen magnificently in the Vedic Hymns and elsewhere among men far advanced in culture.

For this and other reasons, more than one founder of a great religion has at some time turned away from men to nature, and this has renewed his spirit. He that became the Buddha renounced his princely life, and in the forest became the Enlightened One.

Throughout the sacred writings of the Judean faith and the Christian, one is seldom far from nature in its various aspects, homely or sublime—the plowed field, the green pasture, the vineyard; or the wilderness, the desert where the sun smites by day, and men are glad of the shadow of a rock in so weary a land. And in a daring drama never surpassed, the man, Job, is challenged to measure his pride of understanding against that of God who has laid the foundations of the world and sea and holds these in the hollow of his hand; who knows the treasures of the snow, could loose the bands of Orion, and bind the sweet influences of the Pleiades.

Nature gives to talent its materials for craft and science, for art and religion. The mind begins with nature's offer in overflowing generosity, and then adds to it miracle after miracle.

Nature for many, however, is more than a giver of materials. Woodland, lake or rocky headland, for some men, is the only proper place for creative work. So it has been for poets and painters and occasionally even for the mathematician.

IV

Yet, for all this, many, if not most of our originative men work best in or near town or city. And many would prefer it so, even if it were not prescribed for them by their need of laboratory or assistants or for capitalist patron. For they feel the need of friendly counsel and discussion as well as instruments and clerks. And with some the town gives, above all, its stir and spur, its noise and colour, its excitement and rivalry. The day's work goes well, they find, only in such surroundings.

And as to preparation, in the years when youth feels its way toward its chief interest, to skill and power, nature alone is wholly unequal to this high office. Human beings about the youth can bring to him the very breath of his creative life. The family itself may be almost able to give what is needed. Yet even in these rare families something more is almost always required; to be gained by friends, and some manner of schooling; by a bit of absence from home, and trial at one or another kind of work before the final choice. With this, too, self-reliance must be conjoined with the full acceptance and practice, stimulated usually by others, of all those indispensables earlier recorded. The town, it is true, may leave the gifted man home-sick. But Carmel, with its wind-bent pines and ocean, seems as yet not so good a nurse of genius as London. But there is no exclusive choice required. Any one to-day can at will be in town or countryside, having the benefaction both of men and of nature. And for the several kinds of production, so different in their demands upon ability, each may find his own.

INSIGHT AFTER BAFFLED EFFORT

I

A still further service from nature leads us to a fresh field. It is her benefaction to baulked talent. For as though she and Laotse had listened to the same teacher, she invites the disheartened worker after his long fruitless effort to advance by retreating for a while, to gain his end by not seeking it; by turning aside to herself. In this, however, nature is not alone. A like invitation may come from many another source, and give an equal benefit. A few instances will picture what is meant. And first of sleep, and what is close to sleep, as a way past the obstacle.

A student of mine whose prime interest was in mechanics and engineering, told me that after long vain labour at a problem concerned with the diesel engine, he gave up all work on the problem and turned to other things. After some three months of pre-occupation with this different interest and while he was still in the midst of it, there came to him one night in his sleep the solution of the problem he had long dismissed from his thoughts—a solution that stood the test of the clear light of day.

Again, the distinguished agricultural botanist, Albert S. Hitchcock, whose speciality was the study of grasses, told me (on shipboard bound for the Philippines whither he was going for further work on grasses) of an experience of his in South America. It was his custom in the field to gather about thirty specimens of each grass that interested him, each thirty tied into a separate sheaflet, and all taken to his room until he could examine them on another day. One night, after such a day in the field, he dreamed that in one of his little sheaves of the day before, he had by mistake included along with the sort he had recognized, some specimens of a grass of a different sort; he had not seen that it was different. On awaking he examined the particular sheaf, and found that it was as he had dreamed.

And then he added for me a telling fact. The unrecognized grass was by all authorities, not to be found at that latitude in the South American country of his field work, but only much farther south. Evidently, in the gathering, something was seen and marginally impressed on his mind—something whose full meaning was not allowed to develop into clearer judgment. For subconsciously he 'knew' that the plant could not and should not be found there. But in sleep the inhibition, the hindering prejudice from his very erudition, had fallen away, and the actual impressions from the day before could now have their proper intellectual effect.

Close to sleep, but not sleep itself, is the fact that at times a new insight comes when half-awake. Here the mind, hitherto baffled, is both refreshed by the preceding rest and sleep, but also the person's thinking has not, as yet, become entangled in all the intricacies of his besetting ideas about his problem. In his half-slumberous consciousness the whole is freer to take new shape, and intimations too weak to cope with the habitual, now have their chance.

With some, however, the sleepless stretch at night when *trying* to sleep brings the desired insight. These periods were, for Cannon, harvest times. Indeed, it was in one of them he at last saw the clear meaning, simple and single, of the many seemingly unrelated bodily effects of adrenalin that he had discovered. These diverse effects, it now appeared clear, were, from first to last, exactly the bodily changes needed by an animal in a critical situation which requires either fighting or flight.

II

Sleep and its near neighbours, just considered, are, however, but some among many other means by which the mind, long-puzzled, suddenly comes out into the light. An example or two may not be amiss.

The mathematician, Poincaré, when examining a particular area of his specialty, out over the horizon of what then was known in mathematics, came to a point where he made no further progress. Just at this time he joined a geological excursion and while on this expedition, and without any occurrence he could notice in his own mind or outside it to suggest the new arrival, an idea came which was cardinally significant for the advancement of his mathematical problem. On another occasion, while working in a particular field in mathematics which seemed to him disconnected from his previous work, he became disgusted with his failure, went to the seaside, and thought of other things. Here one morning while walking on the bluff, there came to him with sudden and immediate certainty the significant connection between his present baffling work and other work which had seemed so remote from it. Again, when Poincaré was at a standstill having met only one obstacle after another, he went off to his military service. And one day, while walking along a street, the solution of the old problem occurred to him, but he gave no further attention to it. And only at the end of his military service did he again take up the question and found in his mind all the elements he needed; and he had only to put them together; and he wrote out his final memoir at a single stroke.

Thus in Poincaré's case, difficulties that could not be overcome by great effort, disappeared almost of themselves when he ceased to wrestle with them, and turned to other things.

III

Experiences like these are indeed strange. But are they of a kind of which only a few examples are known, as are the lone remnant trees on California's coast? Are they occurrences in the present case only in exceptional men, or men engaged in matters in uncommon fields of interest?

It is true these examples are not ordinary; but every observant person is familiar with instances, though perhaps less striking, in his own experience.

The instances cited were drawn from no single field of work, and examples could have been drawn from a wider range of science.

But what of the fine arts and other creative work? Was it Leonardo da Vinci who at times stared blankly at some shapeless blur on the wall until it grew of itself into some image fit for his work in hand? Crystal-gazing is twin-brother to this odd mode of inviting the soul. And every psychologist to-day is at home in a kindred procedure, of setting before a person he is examining a large ink-blot asking him to gaze at it and tell whatever it may grow into as he stares and stares at it with an empty mind. With several such trials and with a variety of ink-blots, a glimpse may be gained of a person's inner life.

Many of us, finally, may have discovered for himself that after trying for a while fretfully and in vain to recall some well-known name, if only he will give up the attempt, and turn his mind to something else, in the midst of this the missing name enters of itself. I have had so many persons corroborate my own experience of this that I believe it must be a common mode of the mind. Instance could be heaped on instance of the benefit from ceasing all further attempt and turning to something else.

Evidently, then, the insight that comes during or immediately after the relaxing occasion is no product outright of the outer scene; is no mechanical reaction to external situations. The insight comes only to the mind prepared to receive it; comes only as the inner culmination of thought and will, long continued and long aimed toward the illumination. The mind must be prepared to recognize whether what arises is insight and not mirage; that the solution of the problem is actually the solution.

For it is clear that the hard-working mind when driven too hard is subject to something like that which takes place in the hand when it cramps, and can no longer deftly handle the object it holds. So the cramping mind clutches motionless its problem with loss of all delicacy of understanding.

Such occurrences in a particular field of the mind may not be wholly unrelated to the great revolutions in the mind as a whole, which in religion are called conversion, but are not confined to religion. Men, deep in a special kind of business, have told me of a fairly sudden inner revulsion in them which turned them to a different kind of business, or even against business itself and to the life of the scholar. Here, as in religion, there has come a new level of understanding by which the whole scene is transformed, and the will and all the constructive powers turn to a new field and to new tasks. In both the less and the greater change the constructive process itself has quite eluded the person's own attention and announces itself only in the finished product.

FAVOURING WINDS AND HURRICANE

I

Home, school, travel, the situation in which there comes suddenly the answer to a long-troubling question, such factors may properly be called externals, but in large part by discourtesy. For in truth the deep interior of the person must go out to meet them, must consent and give them a hand before they can work their wonders with him.

Another such commanding influence should be mentioned. Some man of uncommon personal power, or a small group of such persons setting one another aglow, prepared to hold aloft an idea more powerful still, can become the authors of a 'cause', a 'movement', perhaps short-lived, perhaps permanently giving a new design of life for a people, an entire civilization. Every kind of learning and of art, every great religion, looks back to such a source; and it deeply affects the productive work of every person in the community into which the movement sweeps.

Every great teacher, of any land or age, has such a power. He brings young and old to a new order of ideas and aims, makes these clear and majestic, and their beholder becomes their servant for life. In my own youth Howison was such a teacher, as was Hopkins of Williamstown to many, and Arnold of Rugby. Socrates, who taught Plato, became the instructor and inspirer for multitudes in many lands through many centuries. Such teachers lay a creative hold not only of the intellect of their hearers, but even more, of their affections and will. A disregard of this larger office of the great teacher is perhaps at the root of Albert Schweitzer's declaration that Jesus was no teacher, instead He takes possession of the whole being of those who really hear Him.

II

There is another manner of entrance into the creative mind and taking possession there which is less personal, less individual, or face to face. It is to be seen wherever many conjointly are carried along as by an invisible power; a wind, often, as of the trades, but at times a hurricane. Men of rare ability as well as plain men may be so much at one with the current that they are persuaded that their motive is wholly initiated and continued from within themselves. In the end they find they are in a fertile and well-watered land, or in a desert with only wreckage about them. Their productive power gains opportunity, or is wasted accordingly.

These social currents acting on talent are of many fields of interest, of mechanics, science or government. In the Italy of the Renaissance, for example, city upon city—Florence, Pisa, Venice, Rome, and all the rest—were in tumult over their daily new achievements in art. In Cellini's writing one sees artists hurrying from studio to studio; in a fine frenzy over what they had just observed, in loud tones praising it or damning it; but never without passionate interest. Painting, sculpture, architecture, the goldsmith's art—all seemed wrought in a fervent heat. Individual inflamed individual; and city, city in appreciation and rivalry. Also in Italy and afar in Europe then and later, what fervour was there for letters, and re-acquaintance and enlargement of humane learning; and for physical science. Erasmus coming to Sir Thomas More, Milton visiting Italy and viewing what the Tuscan artist had there done with his optic glass; while in London, Shakespeare was drawing for his dramas matter from all lands and all times, making England proud and happy in her isle and in her history. And for erudition and fresh discovery, young men, and men well on in years, sought out one another, travelling from land to land; from University to University, with manuscripts, now multiplied by printing—and by fresh reports they learned what was being done with telescope and microscope; reports, too, perhaps, of a youngster who defended the thesis that everything Aristotle taught was false—men set one another afire for all manner of origination. Not until later centuries were there so many powerful currents to carry ability to such varied excellence.

III

For in the centuries following, all these currents continued and to them were added several having no less power.

The interest in material wealth, present wherever there are men, has in our time become a torrent, sweeping toward its own ends more persons and a larger proportion of the world's ability than ever in the story of mankind. Especially is this true in the United States, where other interests than those of business success find it difficult or quite impossible to maintain their due influence on the mind of young and old. Nearly everything in the land speaks for this form of production, this form of success.

And even when youth feels drawn and turns to law or medicine or to architecture, painting, or letters, he is in his productive work often overpowered by its opportunities for gain. And in other lands this sweep of interest is known. Economics has come to be regarded as the only way to the good life, and economic forces are declared to be the chief determining forces in individuals and in the history of peoples.

This creed, this current of interest, has its supreme manifestation in the Russia of our day where revolution was early dominated by zealots of the economic faith. In that immense country, every originative mind now for decades has felt the Revolution's impact; and spreading beyond, this force is felt in every continent, and almost in every man's every waking hour. It compels every productive person and many who are not, to yield to it or resist it, or to choose from its turmoil what he will favour and what he will fight against to the end. Its plan is both broader and narrower than that of the French Revolution; it is far more confident that economics is the key to a Valhalla for Proletarians the world over, more thorough in its methods of compulsion and destruction, readier to turn art, science and religion into tools of the State, and wholly without zeal for either the liberty, or the equality, or the brotherhood of men everywhere. Its early merit that drew to it so many generous minds, was its fierce will for the welfare of the labouring man. Terrible are the means still used after decades to attain this end. Means so terrible they vitiate the very end toward which the movement was aimed.

Through all modern times there has been the current of interest to sustain, cleanse and strengthen the will for the dignity and worth of man. The current's force has been toward something better than the best yet attained in the conduct of men singly and together toward other men; and with effect. For it has almost ended the institution of ownership in human beings, and their purchase and sale, as cattle are bought and sold. In almost every country it has effectively combated the capture and shipment of men for slavery; and serfdom, the sale of land together with the workers on it, has been brought to an end. There has been a continuing fight against the production, manufacture and sale of dangerous drugs, beyond the amount of them required for science and medicine; against the traffic in obscenity in its many forms. And, above all, against the worldwide traffic in women and children.

This moral current is so strong and well-channelled that many who have no faith in any but their own human powers feel its irresistible sweep, and turn their abilities in its direction.

In the fuller current there is concern also for man's relation to the Eternal. A current that for a time had to do chiefly with liberating the individual's conscience from submission to the authority of other men, or any institution of men—this current, in so far as it sweeps a mind with it, works into the very centre of everything a man does: into the product from his factory; into the mind and body of those he heals; into the novel or poem he writes, or into his academic lectures.

No able mind to-day can be unaware of the wide and passionate interest in government. No man to-day, whatever his concern may be—and whether in economics, science, letters, art, morals or religion—can afford to be indifferent to politics. The fate of all men is profoundly shaped by laws and rulers, as Germans and Russians now are aware, and as Scandinavians, Dutch, Swiss, Britons, and Americans have long known.

But it was the French who gave to their concern for government by and for the people the rush and consuming heat of a forest fire. Disruptive, destructive have been some of its consequences to its own country and others, such was its fury; and so deep were the longings it promised to satisfy that men in increasing millions were compelled to decide for or against a form of government pledged to place first the welfare of plain human beings long deprived of what all men need. Since then no nation's constitution, no act of Congress, no poem, drama, or novel can come forth without its maker and its appraisers being aware of a judgment waiting and ready to acclaim or denounce it according to its author's acceptance or rejection of the ruling ideas of that momentous day.

The sweep of this current of thought and desire has, at last, after centuries of mere thought upon the virtual anarchy between nations, the human cost of this anarchy, entered into practical statecraft; in creating the League of Nations, and the World Court; and then, learning from the failure of these, establishing the United Nations. The stream of purpose for the great object these instruments would serve, is drawing a growing number of persons into its tide; but not yet enough. Its force, however, is already so great that no nation anywhere can be unconscious of it, even when ignoring or resisting it.

IV

These and countless other currents flow and swirl around the minds of our era. What has already been said of some particular influence may now be said more assuredly of them as a whole. Few who live to-day, even on the Gobi Desert or the Polar Ice Cap, can remain quite uninfluenced by one or several of these currents. And in the Occident, no form of talent can quite insulate itself from their influence on its goal and the manner of working toward that goal—whether it be in making homes for orphans, or hospitals for the sick; in shaping anew our social imperatives, or our instruments of justice; whether it be in writing, painting, or architecture, in science, philosophy or religion. The winds of interest blow on the apprentice, as well as on the masters of any craft.

Youth, most of all, is subject to these winds. And since each movement has beside its sane centre, its fanatics bent on wild excess, this zeal of the young is both a promise and a threat. For in a mass movement there is some degree of hypnotism with consciences surrendered to a sole suggested interest, a single voice of command. All else is as though it did not exist. Men in battle for the right are in this state of mind; as are also those battling for the wrong. The Hitler Youth, afire for the greatest of Germanys; and Stalin Youth, both in Russia and in many another land, show this hypnotic passion for a particular good at any price. In China of an older day, it was thought that the aged have a favoured access to wisdom. In the West of recent decades, the young have been assured that they above all others see the truth. Either one of these two teachings is as inept as the other; there are both wise and foolish youths among our creators of to-day. Even as there are both wise and foolish among the aged. The art of choosing aright from among the many currents to which one's talent shall be bent is not a gift that comes at any particular age without the asking. It is gained like any other art, by apprenticeship and discipline and dedication to its mastery. It is an art added to the art of the engineer or essayist, of the statesman or etcher, or of any other artificer, by which his skill, taste and knowledge are brought to a fruition that is not bitter.

So great is the power of these currents of interest that affect the producers, it is apt to suggest that the youth preparing for his work, and the prepared worker as well are swept along as leaves by the stream. This is hardly true even of the weakest of us, the least resistant. For even these must in some degree give themselves to the cause they support; approving it, putting their labour and will into its work. Even the best minds never go the whole way, they choose their stopping point, they help to direct the current itself; they make it the servant of their own best purpose. Thus the current here is not wholly external as is the on-rush of a broken dam. The currents that sweep men's minds have to enter into the mind it carries with it; it must find there something congenial to it, ready to accept it, and go with it. The originative mind maintains always some of its initiative, some of its liberty, and requires that the external force offer acceptable terms before the man will consent to go the way proposed.

IV

CREATIVE POWER ITSELF
INGREDIENTS OF ABILITY

1

THE ability to create any of the multitude of valued things earlier in review—wheat fields or baked bread, canoes or ocean liners, hospitals or courts of law, poems or symphonies—is no single ability. No one of these creations of men springs from sheer imagination, as often is said; or of sheer thinking, as it seems to others. When tests of intelligence, such as those of Binet, were at the peak of confidence in them, it seemed to some that by intelligence tests alone geniuses could be discovered. But the after-story of children so selected and labelled failed to confirm this idea.

Indeed, many diverse abilities unite to bring forth novelties of value. Few would doubt this to be true of the Egyptian Pyramids, or China's Great Wall, or Bonneville Dam, or of the *Phaedo* or the Choral Symphony; or the Charter of the United Nations. Such creations require the action of all the chief powers of an individual or of many individuals in common. And so it is also of far less distinguished work. But this to be accepted may need a moment's more consideration.

Into Wordsworth's sonnet beginning

> Milton! thou should'st be living at this hour:
> England hath need of thee;

there went both imagination and thought, but not these only. In Bedlam there is imagination and thinking a-plenty, either running wild, or driven by delusions or morbid self-absorption. In this sonnet, the power of imagery, and of judgment are in the stern control of knowledge—knowledge of the England of Wordsworth's own time, and of Milton's; of Milton's genius and its dedication to his country's welfare in a time of peril. Into the poem there went also a knowledge of many forms of verse, and a pleasure in the one he selected for these noble lines.

And besides his knowledge of his mother tongue, there was also mastery of the special shade, colour and after-glow of each word, each phrase, each sentence. The knowledge, the intelligence, these were supplemented by a sensitiveness to beauty of a hundred kinds—of parts, of the whole, of impression, form and meaning. Quiet emotion, and affection also did their work; and over all was a controlling purpose to create what would awaken in others some echo of the pleasure, and pain and regret that had been experienced in shaping the art-work itself.

Or, turn to a contrasting work, the Campanile that looks out through the Golden Gate. Its making required a no less wide range of powers—virtually all the chief powers of mind of a gifted man, a man specially trained in the use of those powers. Judgment and knowledge were employed, but in a somewhat different field and for a partly different end. The poet in John Galen Howard went into the design, but with a rigorous discipline in architecture, and a love of Giotto's Tower, and a purpose to transfer this to a new time and new surroundings. Its granite, its marble, its steel must sustain a weight and bells, and stand against storm, and recurring earthquake. The poet, the artist must consult with engineer, with the geologist; and his design must be made to fit into an inclusive design for many other buildings. All that was in the man went into the work—his eye, hand, and brain; his memory and foresight, his feeling of pleasure and pain. His affection and emotion, his sentiment, his impulses—all these schooled his purpose.

There would be no reader's patience here for illustrations ranging through the achievements in the Valley of the Tennessee and in California, to the latest word of science, technology and manufacture. But we should find by a wider survey, I am confident, that while, as in Mozart, some special rarity of endowment was an essential factor, yet even here the gift was complex, and the finished product came out of this complexity conjoined with many abilities beside; and that generally the product springs out of no simple single gift. Rather it issues from a determined purpose and a practical exercise of several, if not all, large interlacing abilities.

II

Creative power, as has just been said, is not a particular power, one among many others. It is rather a concerted action of many fundamental abilities—the ability to imagine, and think; to feel pleasure and pain; to love and hate, and to urge body and mind into action to attain a chosen end. These abilities properly united and directed suffice. Is every man, then, a creator? Yes, in some degree, potentially, but often he is asleep, distracted or unurged to bring forth what is within his powers. The adage 'necessity is the mother of invention' suggests what is the fact.

An experiment ingeniously contrived by Dr. Kate Gordon Moore attests that the necessity may be such only in a Pickwickian sense. One day, to the dismay of her college students, young men and women, she required of them an invention, to be brought in at some generously distant but definite day ahead. Some were dumbfounded, many were loud in protest: 'I am not an inventive genius'; 'I have no talent for invention'; 'I know I can't'; 'It's useless even to try'; 'It's unjust.' This was the gist of their first reaction. But, she made it clear, she asked for no feat of Watt or Edison, but only for some simple device to meet some simple need in their own experience. The barricades were abandoned; the rioters went home. And at the appointed time virtually every mother's son and daughter of them brought in an invention never known in the universe until then. Under so persuasive a despot I have no slightest doubt, these cubs would have brought forth any other kind of novelty she'd name. For she would have named only what was within their common endowment, their common experience and training. They would not have produced counterparts of the Mahabarata, or the sacred precincts of Nikko.

Many of these youths would have failed, I fear, if pressed to do whatever demanded the use of more than the bare rudiments of those higher powers, essential to the sonnet, the campanile, and essential also to much of science, of justice through law, of painting and drama, of obligation, and of confidence beyond sight and logic.

In the master, these powers are not strangers that have at last been befriended and made one's own. They are old powers made new; biological abilities re-empowered with skill and strength and honour, and offered novel objects on which to act and around which to play. Their roots are in man's natural endowment, but transformed by many a device of culture, even as natural flint stones rounded by ice and water are still further shaped by early man into tools for his own peculiar use.

And this elevation of man's biological abilities is of no recent beginning. It is found in many a still-backward people, who, one finds, are not always occupied in anger, cupidity, hunger, thirst and lust, but are aware of beauty and often pass on into awe and reverence in the presence of the sunrise, of snow-storm and lightning, and all the voices of the forest, the mountains and the sky.

These higher powers come only by the fresh upward reach of individuals seeking to exceed what is attained and valued in the world of to-day, of yesterday and of all earlier years. Santayana speaks of experiences deeper than those of clear scientific ideas—experiences which spring from the variety of this world with its strange revelations and mystic loves, the experience, too, of sin. Rufus Jones, Reinold Niebuhr, and many another also speak of these higher powers not wholly palsied in a people pre-occupied with lesser things. In Homer, this realm repeatedly appears simply in the query about a man, as though the answer would tell his very substance, 'Is he kind to strangers, and reverent toward the gods?'"

Creative power, then, is no gift to the few. It is in every man. It is distinctly human—a spiritual use of his plain human endowment.

III

Some further truths about the mind of every person should be stated—in repetition of what has appeared earlier in this writing and perhaps to be said again later. They are of moment in awakening a rightful expectancy of what can come of man's power. His work will hardly suffer by knowing more of his own mind and of the minds of his fellow-men to whom his product is addressed—whether this product be a novel, a drama; a painting or a dwelling; food or clothes.

The generosities of men are as solid a part of men's natural structure as are their cupidities and cruelties. Nor are these generosities weaklings. They are potent, able to hold their own, and indeed to gain ground against their opposites. No community in health could continue without these masterful powers. Crass self-seeking is there, but held within bounds, and indeed often is made to serve man's generous common aims. All who would take part in gratifying these sturdy impulses cannot afford to believe that a genuine regard for others is a delusion contrived to hide from us the distasteful fact that man's only interest is self-interest and nothing else. The truth is that sympathy is no less real than antipathy, love than hate. Man by nature is both social and solitary, both co-operative and quarrelsome. Each of these opposites is supple, pliable, subject to strengthening or enfeebling by continued united effort. Prussia's history speaks of the one direction of effort; modern Sweden's of the other.

Again, man, for all his kinship with the animals, is far above the highest animals—as far above as are the animals above the plants. He is better endowed than animals, and his animal endowment itself he can use—in civilized communities he does use—for aims and toward results which have no place in the life of animals. Man is led from within to self-criticism, to self-condemnation, to desire and labour for new surroundings, a new society and new men. Productive work in art or economics or politics, that takes no account of this, libels men and misses the mark.

Further, sex, powerful though it is, is not the all-mastering power it is often thought to be. Some individuals are under its absolute rule, but not men generally. Instead, sex is but one among a number of powerful human promptings or desires, some of which are even more imperious than sex. Men soon die if their desire for food and water is not heeded; die also if any of several other bodily needs are not met. In contrast, men and women can, and often do, lifelong, leave their procreative impulses ungratified, without serious harm. And among the less specific organic impulses, self-interest dogs our every step, and only with immense difficulty and often with but small success, do we keep it to heel. When it comes to a pitched battle between self-interest and sex—self-interest, in the form of greed, of social ambition, or personal liberty, can require sex to assist these or at least not to obstruct them. These other interests have power to delay or exclude their rival. The attempt to make them merely variants, or sublimations of the sexual *libido* seems reckless of the plain evidence.

DIVERSE COMPLEMENTS OF TALENT

Like their portraits, men of ability as just seen, are in several respects alike; their minds have a common structure, a manner of working. But no less is it true that each is evidently himself and none other. The wonder of individuality, however, must not detain us, as it has others through the centuries, nor should one here attempt to tell of unnumbered degrees of ability, from weak-mindedness to genius; nor of those contrasts among gifted persons by which the powers in some are on the verge of turmoil, if not of civil war—as with Coleridge, Poe, and Wilde; while with others—Franklin, Darwin, Tennyson, Lincoln and hundreds more—their powers are held safely in order, are under government.

The characters of Theophratus, and the very different classic four temperaments—sanguine and melancholic, phlegmatic and choleric—may distantly suggest the region now to be visited, in a manner, I fear, hardly better than that of the breathless tourist bent on acquaintance in an afternoon with all in some notable town.

I

By the direction of their creative interest, by something that includes curiosity and more, persons differ as do white and black and the greys between. Having strange differences of constitution, natural and acquired, men confront a universe no whit less diverse than themselves—of the sun by day, and the moon and stars by night, of woods, rivers, and mountains; of men, women, and children; of talk and laughter; of fear, anger and affection.

CREATIVE POWER ITSELF 75

All these and more beyond naming appear and disappear in the ever-changing scene. And a man may notice them all, but all inertly, not yet fascinated by them. Until at last the lens of his mind is focused, and much that is outside the distinct field is blurred and lacks interest. And what objects are chosen—in this the individuality of men appears. Each finds his own field and in it the material for his craft and the starting point for the thrust of his inventive will.

But the interest of many a person focuses itself not on any concrete object whole and complete, but on aspects, on abstractions from this fullness—on the colour, hardness, and form of minerals, or on their chemistry or geology. And even when men turn this attention to the same narrow and abstract aspect of things, they reveal most divergent interests in considering it and in dealing with it. Helmholtz, Wagner, and Bell, for example, alike turned intently to *sound*, and applied talent to it, with the strangest contrast in results—a treatise on Sensation of Tone, *The Flying Dutchman*, and all its rich company, and the Telephone.

Or, to return to what is concrete, the human scene, yet viewed with opposite interests, persons make of it, severally, a novel or a painting, a new chapter in psychology or in ethics, or a political revolution.

For the moment let us ask none of a score of questions as to the character and source of these differences of interest, but merely acknowledge their existence, and that by them men turn the mind as to different constellations in the sky, or in the mountains to the tracks of deer, or writing of ice on granite, to moss on sugar-pine, or the snow-peak.

II

Individuality has other contrasts. There is the contrast between the *serene* disposition and the *dour*, with all gradations between. Emerson would represent the golden end of this scale with his mind's dwelling-place less clouded, less troubled than that of Olympus, and more like that of Parnassus. And Carlyle would represent the opposite, his habitation of mind more constantly in dark vapours than was his Chelsea, which though near

London's fog, sees many a sunny day. Serenity, even gladness, attends the talent of some and redoubles their power; while others are weighted down and halted by lead on feet and heart. The plays of Ibsen, the Kalavala of the Finns, and many a Russian novel have over them no little of this unnerving gloom.

For it is now well known that the different emotions may have opposite effects on the mind as well as on the body. Anger, and moderate fear, for example, may be strength-giving, sthenic; while despondency and some forms of fear are weakening, asthenic. And it seems clear that some persons are by disposition prepared for the one or the other of these opposite types of emotion, which have their contrasting effect on both the quality and the amount of the person's production; favouring those normally serene or even glad, and frowning upon those of low spirits.

But, as already suggested, any of these contrasts of disposition or temperament is named commonly by its extremes, and says nothing exact about the multitude between, who also may pour out fruits of their talent. For even the immortals, who may at times have tasted either ecstasy or despair, could hardly have had either of these as their work-a-day level. That mighty labourer, St. Paul, had seemingly but once a sight of what was not lawful to utter; and on that day did none of his mighty deeds. For commonly the mind labours best in mid-zone, when one only remembers and is not experiencing the heights or the depths of the spirit.

Even the poets—whom some have regarded as unfit for their office unless steeped in melancholy—commonly are not so. Homer and Virgil are not so, nor are Dante and Shakespeare. Browning knew the night, but did not make it the place of his abode. And with most men who bring forth what enriches our social life, our statecraft, our architecture and science, it is as with Trollope who went to his daily stint of writing regardless of mood or special inspirational elation. These men live and work usually not far from the mean. They find a quiet satisfaction in their task; they from time to time are disappointed but not crushed when things go wrong; and when all goes well they go on encouraged, sthenically excited, but not for long are they elated.

III

Another important contrast is between those bound by many ties of sympathy—with persons, places and events—and those ruled by sentiments that detach them from most of what lies beyond themselves. On the one side are men generous in spirit, of out-flowing appreciation, even of affection, far and wide. On the other side are mortals who look out on all the varied scene with mild antipathy, or even a sneer. At the one extreme would be Francis of Assisi who found in everything his brother, be it wolf or leper; and created a great fellowship of men. And at the opposite extreme would be those eremites who found in all the world around them little or nothing but what menaced their love of God.

Much can be created under the rule of either of these contrasting dispositions. Buddhism—to speak not of its varied sects, but only of its primal spirit—included a studied detachment from all that men commonly prize or desire; not only riches and place and power, but even individuality, even personality itself. There is pity, a form of love, outgoing to all the world, but with a feeling of worth in none of its particulars, but only in the One in which these disappear. Yet this detachment became the foundation of a world religion.

On a nearly opposite foundation there was erected another world religion, Christianity, on *attachment* to persons and their relations with one another, as having in them eternal worth. And with this went the practical aim to free men and their society from their evil, and create of them a divine community, with a Divine Person at its head.

But while either of the two dispositions comports with immense production, they are not alike in what is created under their auspices. Buddhism and Christianity have each their distinct qualities of product, despite all that is theirs in common. The institutions, for example, which each finds most congenial by reason of its fundamental attitude toward persons and their mundane affairs differ widely, as do also the types of individuality most favoured in the two faiths. Or to leave religion for lesser matters fostered by the opposite tempers, of warm sympathy and detachment, one may recall some of the writings of Stevenson, and beside them some of the work of Santayana; or the products of Dickens beside those of Henry James—not to speak of those whose detachment moves over into satire, cynicism, disgust with all the offerings of experience.

IV

The utterly social and the utterly rebellious, let them be the last of these contrasts in personality to be considered. At the one pole is the man who lives and breathes in the minds of those about him, like the character in Henry James's story, who mysteriously ceased to exist, body and soul, when not in society. In the neighbourhood of this extreme are your complete conformists· those who praise things as they are. At the other pole is the person at inner war with the life about him and with whatever in himself mirrors that life. He and his fellow-warriors see all custom—to echo John Stuart Mill—as a despot in ceaseless antagonism to human advancement. The mind in rebellion against the despotism came into its own in the French Revolution, and thence to Russia and Germany, with some of its kind now in every land. Not of their temper, but yet on their side of centre, are the many liberal minds, cherishing their independence, their criticism of much that is customary.

At its worst the one pole holds the satisfied conformist who sees no need of change, and who consequently lacks motive to be creative. And at the other pole at its worst are those who see no good in what now exists, and who use all their powers for clearance of ancient rubbish, for destruction, and in their zeal for this are likewise uncreative. The destructive use of creative power is tenfold easier and, for many, tenfold more exciting than is laborious upbuilding. This destructive use of human power is especially tempting to the impatient, the undisciplined. To some it would seem that Samson's greatest achievement was the ruin of Dagon's temple. To many, the rebellious Satan stands first in *Paradise Lost*. At or near this extreme is found no small part of the painting, sculpture, novel writing and the politics of recent decades.

But, happily, the far larger company of the talented of our time and of other times are less intemperate. They are far from unlimited conformity and no less far from nihilistic opposition to all custom to all actual achievements. The idea that custom is the unremitting adversary of human advancement seems to these moderates but a specious half-truth. Socrates was no nihilist, no anarchist; he was in 'the loyal opposition'.

And in our own time was Abraham Lincoln, destroyer, defender, rebuilder, one of the most constructive persons that ever came forth from his nation.

v

Creative persons thus have some portion of their individuality in their differing possession of a vast variety of features of mind, of which but a few have just been named—the different direction of their predominant interest; their position in the long line running between the serene and the overcast; between all-inclusive sympathy and all-exclusive detachment; and, finally, between utter conformity and utter rebellion.

And what in closing should be said of the peculiar quality of the contrasts considered in this chapter?

The contrasts of individuality just noted seem reasonably to be close to that important kind we know as attachment or affection, which, according to the character of the objects claiming the attachment do much to distinguish one maker from another, and to bestow on the products of each their contrasting qualities and worth. And of these matters more will be said at once.

THE ATTACHMENTS AND PURPOSES OF THE MAN

Above all (in closing this part of our account of Creators), the man's power is controlled by what he loves. Whatever holds fast his affection must hold fast also his thought; and around it his memories will gather and his imagination will play. The object of his attachment will be the storm centre of his passions; fear and anger will arise when it is threatened; joy when gifts flow in to it; sadness when it is lost. The man's talents are at its service. His purpose sets into activity all that he has—to understand it, and give it sway.

I

The products of men declare the immense range of what holds their affections. And from a hurried recall of a few main features of the scene viewed earlier, there may emerge large differences of fact that to some persons can hardly fail to seem differences, not in fact only, but in worth—in the worth of the things made, and of the affections which led to their making.

It was seen that men add to their physical surroundings, and otherwise so transform them that they live in what is largely a new environment, of highways, railways, airways, docks, and warehouses, office buildings and dwellings—all lighted, heated, and empowered by human art, itself set a-work by the desire for such things and the love of them.

In no whit less measure do men take their social surroundings in hand, and by language, laws, courts, and police, and able government join tribes, join clan to clan; abolish some of the worst of social institutions—such as private blood-vengeance, slavery, and serfdom—and bring into existence the immense city, the immense nation, the empire. These have come of men's talents, driven by the love of such achievements, and the will to bring them into being, in spite of the loves and hates that resist.

And with all this and more, men re-make themselves and others—not always for the worse, as some cynics may say—but commonly for the better. For in every nation in health, the most of men have been brought to a far wider loyalty, to a far greater company of men than in the tribe, the clan. The most of men become free from much of their ill-will and have in them good-will to a company numbered by millions, within and beyond their nation's border. And in each such company men act and *prefer* to act toward one another without violence, and under law. And in all such nations with all there is of avarice, and self-will, many, if not most men, long for a juster national life, a juster international life; and they will gradually, it is hoped, down the obstacles to these and set their purpose to attain them.

Such is the one appearance of the scene, with its three regions of actual play of originating power. And corresponding with each region was desire for change there, or if change came without forethought, then an appreciation of it, a love of it, and the will to preserve and increase it.

And now to a different point from which the scene appears traversed by quite different dividing lines.

II

Men find spread before them for their affection and effort several kinds or levels of existence, to any one of which they may become chiefly attached and there do their main work.

The first of these is the level of existence which we men share with the higher animals, where life asks of us and them alike that we obtain air, meat and drink, clothing, shelter and defence, activity, rest and mating. A few men in any civilized community live merely as animals. They are hardly creative at all, save as animals procreate. None, however, can live entirely within the region of breathing, eating and sleep. But, while holding to this, men commonly add to it a freer domain with more air, more view.

A level of being that is slightly above the purely animal, is that in which are produced more abundant, more accessible, more attractive objects for their animal needs, and in more attractive surroundings—the meal is graced with a clean cloth; knife, fork and spoon keep fingers out of the dish. Graces of manner at table make the act of eating less distressing to the eye. The food and drink is prepared with heed for its colour, savour and flavour. In clothing, utility is joined with appearance. And so also of the bed, the hearth, the roof-tree and the garden where flowering plants 'unprofitably gay' are set apart from turnips and onion. Especially in the wedding does man surround the animal impulse with beauty of colour and music, with gifts and rejoicing, with pledges of mutual solicitude and fidelity. In all this array men generally refuse to lose their heart in the purely biological function. They declare themselves attached to something more congenial to another mode of life.

III

On a third level of man's marvellous life, his attachment and purpose—while not rejecting the interests of the two levels just described—include also a region beyond the concern of even the highest animals and is peculiarly or characteristically human. In this region, men are concerned with more than the biological utility of their body and mind, and of the objects round about them merely as these are; but consciously enjoy them, and re-make them to wider use and enjoyment. Voice and language are now made into art, into poetry and dateless wondertales, and lyric song and choral. And there is the music of violin, harp and organ, and full orchestra; and there is the dance, and comedy and tragedy. And much that is great in science is for the joy—not in the quest alone, but still more—in its profound and amazing disclosures. Indeed, in whatever is done to surprise men or make them laugh, or weep, or wonder, both the maker and the beholder rejoice in the product and in the power thus to invent, discover and create. Thus it is with Foucault's pendulum; with the spinning top grown into a gyroscope; the first rude steam engine, the first recognition of an unknown satellite of one of the planets; or of a new element taking its name from Uranus or Pluto. And, to come nearer home, so is it with the latest quip from some Vermont farmer; or when one hears anew an old-remembered song; or reads for the first time *Cyrano de Bergerac, The Happy Prince,* or *Revolt in the Desert.*

In all this region, men give the heart not to their bodily hunger and thirst, or their lust, or the call of their unused or over-used muscles; or their impulses for sleep, or their herd impulse. Instead they find themselves in love with their own abilities; with the many things of nature and their own rich additions to all these. It is a wide realm for his labour and delight.

IV

The fourth level is of that life in any people of any time, when men still care for and set their will for what is good at the three levels already noted, but who subordinate all these to the objects of another attachment and of another direction of purpose. They would fulfil as much as may be the intimations of the perfect.

Schweitzer in Africa, signally illustrates in our day this level of creative purpose with his rare union of talents in scholarship, in organ music (especially in his understanding of Bach), in scientific medicine, and in Christian devotion, amid dire hardship; lending all these gifts to the care of a despised and wronged people, in body and spirit. Kagawa in Japan is another high example, under our very eyes, his years in the crowded worst of Kobe's slums, with its hunger, disease and crime. He came to understand and more than understand the poor of Japan, and the impact on them of her industrialists, her militarists with their political ambitions, and directed all his powers to their relief.

At this level are men most diversely engaged. Kant, driven by his affection and will, and not alone by his pure intelligence, showed another form of living. And Socrates and Plato showed still other forms. In politics there were Gladstone, Wilson and Masaryk; in journalism there were Scott of the *Manchester Guardian*, and Ochs of the *New York Times*. And there were philosophers and teachers—to speak only of our own land—Howison, James and Royce. And in letters there run a long line from the recent past, Tennyson, Browning, Thompson. All these and a multitude more have worked and are working in the highlands of the mind.

Of their company, too, are those who wrote the Republic, and Utopia, or who spoke to their own people and among strangers, doing what they could to make of the individual and of the society of individuals something more befitting man's great habitat, with its vast reaches out through the unimaginable distances of dimmest stars, and the unimaginable past, before our earth departed from our sun. In our habitation under the sky, now starred and now sunlit, or with magic clouds—these make report through our very eyes and ears; as do also the ocean and its strong headlands, and the forests of long memory; the mountains that have kept watch through ages before men saw them and stood to pay silent homage to the spirits that must dwell amid such grandeur. And now for long it has been the desire of many to re-make themselves and others into some measure of the stature of spirit befitting also what he knows to lie within him as yet unrealized.

And among the great originators have been many possessed by their idea of the perfect, who yet have sought diligently with help of others (to use the words of our Constitution) to make it more perfect, to amplify those aspects that stand the test of men's reason and conscience, and their highest allegiance.

To some, however, this idea even when cleansed and enlarged appears to be a contrivance of man's own skill of mind and nothing more. But to very many the idea and the allegiance to it, while indubitably of man's making, is also his response to intimations of reality beyond himself; of a mind greater and better than his own, whose majesty at once shames and dignifies and cherishes men and invites them to become fellow-workers in its creative purpose.

V

These levels on which work is done are not impossible to hold to, all of them at once in the one worker. But while this is not impossible, it also is not easy. For they tend to be rivals of one another, as may be illustrated, although from a different field. William James, says his biographer Perry, was predisposed against anything that stressed technique at the expense of subject matter, surface at the expense of depth, or evil at the expense of good. So it might be said of the four levels just considered, each must receive its due accent and no more. And the reader may incline to hold with the writer against anything that stresses the less among the four at the expense of what is greater. In stressing the less, the product then, whether it come from some manufacturer or jurist or poet, will speak with a false accent.

THE SECOND PART

*

Destroyers and Creators

V

ABILITY TURNS DESTRUCTIVE

DISHONOUR IN THE HOMELAND AND BEYOND

I

WE have long been observing the creative use of ability. Yet in the back of our minds all the while the destructive use of human ability has been clamouring for attention. And to this we should now turn. For in every country, men are found who waste their powers, or use them to obstruct themselves or others, or to destroy what has cost the labour of centuries.

There will be no attempt here to trace a hundredth part of all the devious ways men follow in their injury of their fellows. Instead, let us take a particular manner of behaviour that we can see and touch, and about which there is a fair agreement that it is destructive and discreditable. I mean, the violence of men against men and against what men make and love. This manner of action is portentous, and calls imperatively for all that is in us of constructive skill to displace it with what is rightly prized.

A sharper understanding of violence (to which some later chapters will be devoted) is of value in itself; and further, if we should by good fortune find the chief source of this one kind of behaviour, we may have found the source of other kinds of behaviour that are not violent at all, and yet are no less truly destructive.

In America one sees delinquency among youth, and crime among adults as a corrupt flood. Violence abounds in our disputes between managers and the men they employ. Our Coloured citizens are daily and terribly the victims of the pride and power of the Whites. And, largely from the stubborn holding of Negroes as slaves, there was a Civil War between Whites and Whites themselves of the one Nation; perhaps the bitterest and bloodiest of all the civil wars of history.

A proud and powerful people, in some important respects a nation of idealists, has allowed all this to be, as though it came on by fate, and as though the best in the nation was powerless against it all. The whole sorry picture is an insult to the country's intelligence and will. And other countries in so far as they suffer a like disorder share in the insult.

II

The violence of nation against nation is the world's supreme misuse of creative power. For in this violence, men's greatest gifts are turned with horrible understanding to continent-wide desolation. The deep dishonour of it is shared by nearly all nations, but mainly by the Great Powers; and now that the United States is the most powerful of these, theirs is the largest share both of the responsibility and the disgrace.

There cannot here be any telling of war, to bring us face to face with its immensity, of its destruction in every realm that men hold precious. The reader already has wide knowledge of this, so recently has the world been through the most devastating of wars, so vivid has been the reporting of its battles, so lately have the soldiers come home from the horror of it, so many have not come home and never will. And yet, something must be said of it, if only to renew in our minds the indignity of such misuse of human talent. And the indignation that may be aroused is not for its own sake, as sentiment, but to prepare us for renewed thought and purpose to clear us and others from the continuance of this waste and worse than waste of human ability.

We cannot, by dollar signs and long lines of figures, comprehend war's waste—the billions on billions spent on preparation for two world wars, the more billions on waging these wars, and the billions upon billions already spent and still to be spent for decades to come, in restoring but a fraction of what was destroyed; and along with all this we begin once more the weary cycle by pouring out more billions lest still another war find us unprepared.

There is the destruction of the products of men's purpose, their property—shipping, and harbours, docks and warehouses;

ABILITY TURNS DESTRUCTIVE

railways and highways; dams and reservoirs and power-stations; coal mines, oil-wells and iron-mines; furnaces and foundries; farms, crops and granaries; factories of a hundred kinds, with storehouses of materials and finished products. And besides these, there are destroyed office buildings, hospitals, schools, social halls, theatres, churches and homes—indeed, whole villages, towns and whole cities. And worse than this waste of money is the destruction of millions of human lives, and the life-long maiming of other millions in mind as well as body. For in total war toward which all the great powers are now moving, there is psychological warfare which does its best to destroy the social bonds within neighbour nations, and indirectly returns to damage the minds of the country's own citizens. And the best of them become ready to do the very deeds which they have abhorred when done by their enemies.

Violence between nations and within nations thus insults the creative mind in us all. Nothing in our day equals it in the magnitude of its waste and perversion and destruction of the best that we have. Violence within every nation really is creative power squandered in injuring men, and distracts much of the whole community's constructive energy into mere quieting of disorder, and defence against still greater damage. And international violence is now so immense a menace to the whole world that millions of creative minds can do nothing else than invent, discover and organize for destruction. A thousand deep needs go neglected; a thousand great gifts to humanity must remain ungiven. Eminent achievement, as has been seen, requires an orderly growth of communal life, and a wide co-operation of individuals and communities. The nations instead are living in discord, with wreckage of communities all about them; where freely conceived co-operation is more and more difficult. What can be a more urgent enterprise than squarely to face and down this common wrong? *It must be destroyed!*

VI

AN EXPEDITION AND ITS OUTCOME

CONFLICTING REPORTS BY EARLIER EXPLORERS

WE should be the happier if those working against violence could be guided by more assured knowledge of this field. But the voices that should give direction to our thought and conduct, while being by no means contradictory are yet multitudinous and unconcerted as at an afternoon tea.

Let us have some instances of this diversity—in regard to violence.

I

And first of violation of law by our boys and girls. Here we have the services of the police, probation officers and other social workers. Often there are detention homes, 'foster homes', schools for correction or re-education. In not a few places there are juvenile courts with psychologists and psychiatrists to advise the judges. Playgrounds in town and places of recreation, for use day and night, are not infrequent. The means of prevention and cure are thus many and varied, but are far from completely successful.

And as to the causes of the evil, the judgments of experts are hardly less varied. Among the causes given is the insufficient number, training and equipment of the agencies just mentioned. Often the source of the trouble is believed to be the broken home —broken by poverty, or ignorance, by unemployment, alcohol or vice—leaving the household but an empty shell of what is needed for the child, the youth. Or in the unbroken home the boy or girl is repressed, frustrated, and in compensation becomes violently aggressive.

And in the thought of many who have studied the problem of delinquency's causes—the slum; itself an expression of economic processes, and the cure for delinquency is clearly, many persons believe, in correcting these faulty processes.

As for the crime of adults the procedure is with a different emphasis. The offender is arrested, if possible, tried and if convicted, is imprisoned, often with opportunities to learn, at lathe or bench, some skill, or from class or books some wider understanding. Into all this goes much experiment, much thought and patience. Yet it is unequal to the need; our society is ill protected; many an offender goes uncaught, or if found and not punished, too often offends again and again.

The explanation of crime is like that of delinquency, with the thought, well-supported by evidence, that crime for the most part is a continuation of delinquency into adult life. Here, as with delinquency, an important role is assigned to economics. And for the cure many look with hope to the abolition of poverty in the home, along with better criminal laws, better enforced by better courts, and a wiser administration of prisons.

II

The violence which so often attends our disputes between employed and employers in industry and beyond, is answered by no concerted and curative judgment in the community. The violence is clamorously excused or condemned; arrests may be made, concessions agreed upon or refused. Boards, committees and commissions try to mediate or arbitrate. Proposed changes in law are debated, and defeated or adopted. At times the violent are held in check by police and even by soldiers. On the whole, more appeasement, or more restraint seems our chief resource. There are excellent books and addresses on the subject. But there is no clear agreement as to the cause of the violence nor as to the wisest way to end it.

Between the several races in our country—Whites, Negroes and Orientals—the not infrequent violence is both deplored and approved. There are laws, courts and police to protect and punish, and with some success when these are reinforced by public shame and indignation. Lynching has become less frequent, but bodily assault on those of the coloured races, and the destruction of their property are still with us. Several cities with a relatively large number of Negroes have, in their homicide rate, more than Chicago at its worst; and these homicides have included many killings of Negroes by Whites. And, similarly, where there are many Orientals in our country, the treatment for violence between the races is apt to be more violence, more restrictions, more measures, to make the Orientals know and accept an inferior place.

The treatment of our riots, 'rebellions' and our Civil War has not been based on any general and accepted explanation of all these occurrences. The historians explain in their special ways each of these by itself and often with particular causes for each one, but these explanations often differ widely—an objection and resistance, for example, to the Government's collection of taxes in Massachusetts; the objection of military draft in New York City; to the spread of pro-slavery influence in Kansas, or to slavery itself; and, in the North, to the South's economic advantage from its cheap labour, its armed attack on a Fortress of the Union, and of the effort of certain States to secede from the Union.

The treatment of the difficulty that led finally to the Civil War included various efforts in the press and on the platform, in Congress and outside of it. But in the mind of the nation, distracted by conflicting views on slavery and States' rights, the country's practical course was finally to meet force with superior force, as in all the lesser outbreaks of violence by mob or rebels, and to compel obedience to the authority of Government.

III

The greatest of all violence—that of international war—has in the past been treated in many ways, but chiefly by attaining a national armed power great enough, if possible, to defeat, punish and weaken the adversary; and thereafter to maintain a clear superiority over him or any other probable enemy. Century after century has seen some great power achieving a kind of security in this manner, a security against defeat, although not at all against war itself. Thus Persia, Assyria, Egypt, Rome—each for a time maintained itself by victorious violence. France, Germany, Austria, Russia, Japan and the United States have set their wills, each to defeat violently whatever violence might oppose its will. The smaller nations, for the most part, have lived armed and trembling under the protection of a powerful neighbour, somewhat as in a feudal system. Even with many a secondary device against international violence—diplomacy, alliance, arbitration, international law, conferences and congresses—this violence has become rapidly more and more furious and devastating.

Late in the nineteenth century there were attempts at concord by limiting armaments; and there was created a standing Court of Arbitration, followed—after the First World War—by the League of Nations and the Permanent Court of Justice. Monstrous arming soon followed, and in its train a still more monstrous war. And now, in the midst of the wreckage of that war, we have created the United Nations, collectively to keep the peace by military, economic, judicial, educational, and other means. Nothing adequate is yet provided for dealing with any Great Power that has the will for aggression.

IV

Such is the variety of treatment of the world's great scourge. And it corresponds with the variety of belief as to the cause of world violence. And the treatment is the more confused because so many are convinced that the causes are ineradicable, and therefore the disease itself cannot be cured.

Thus, many hold that wars arise from our very nature, from our inborn instinct to fight, to destroy our enemies, so necessary in the struggle for existence. In war, it is believed, men are but obeying 'nature's first law', that of survival, of self-preservation; wars are inevitable; you cannot change human nature.

Others would explain wars by the crowd-like, herd-like character of our collective behaviour. Each nation, on this account, when in deadly danger from without, acts—not sensibly, not rationally, but as a panic-stricken audience in a burning theatre, or as a herd stampeded toward a precipice. We must accept this ugly fact, some believe, and with it recurring wars.

From another quarter come voices declaring that war is an upheaval from the Unconscious, from depths below our observation and our conscious will.

The historians, in contrast, speak confidently of particular events or trends, and individuals in the nation's past—of Prussia's Frederick the Great and his aggressive aims; Bismarck and his practice-wars against Denmark and Austria, thus making ready for his victorious war of 1870, and for a United Germany; leading with many other forces, on to Wilhelm II, the First World War and his defeat, then to Hitler and his war and all the unutterable horrors never to be erased from the world's memory. And since it is well-nigh impossible to counteract these continuing historic forces, dark indeed, in the mind of these believers, is the prospect for the cure of war.

From the economists, in turn, one hears much about war's origin in conflicts of interest in regard to raw materials, production, and markets; in regard to good harbours and the control of trade routes by sea; about nations that have these in abundance and other nations that have them not; about nations whose population exceeds the means of subsistence and therefore must take their neighbours' territory by arms or else starve. In general, the economists' explanations are heard with favour and yet opposite explanations are offered by other specialists.

V

Even these scant illustrations of what is being done and thought of to cope with violence at home and abroad will, I believe, suffice to show the uncertainty, the disagreement, the scattered effort we must meet as we enter this domain to bring it into order. In none of the several provinces in this realm of violence, from youthful crime to war between nations is there the confident intelligent skill with which the surgeon removes diseased tissue, or the officer of public health puts an end to his city's typhus fever.

Nor can we rightly ascribe this ill-success in dealing with violence to our politicians and the benighted public they mislead. For neither the government nor the people can wisely turn for guidance to experts whose opinions are nearly as many as the experts themselves.

The situation is grave to a world of men who are so inventive, so laden with discovery and results in other regions. The destruction of property, the invasion of rights, the assaults on life are human doings, in our midst, before the very eyes of scientists, who eagerly give their years to things that in comparison are trifling, or to matters that, while momentous, increase, not diminish the perplexities of living with one another. A least fraction of that interest that produced the most destructive of all war instruments should now belatedly be directed, let us hope, to the understanding of men's will to destroy one another. In the meantime, the reader will perhaps be less impatient of a fresh effort to reduce by a little the confusion, and increase our understanding in this realm of human conduct, lest it utterly destroy us. The search calls for labour and forbearance; but, with perhaps a tinge of adventure and refreshing outlook. In the end, I believe we shall have things of worth in our hands.

THE HEADWATERS OF TURBULENCE WITHIN THE NATION

I

We have been hearing the divergent reports of explorers in one or another of the many areas of violence, but little or nothing to bring before us the dark region as a whole. Many of us, dissatisfied and curious to see with our own eyes, may be ready to join an expedition intended to traverse at first only that portion of the wilderness that lies within the nation's border, and only after some understanding of things seen there, shall we push on into the ever-deeper wilds where nations fight with nations. In each region our search will be, not for the occasions close at hand that bring disorder, but for the distant, hidden sources of them. Indeed, it is not impossible that in spite of their contrasting appearance, there may be one common source of them all.

II

Now a ready misunderstanding in regard to the divergent reports from those who have studied delinquency or crime, economic conflicts or onslaughts of race on race, should be prevented. To speak of a confusion of tongues of the experts in this region, does not mean any oversight or misprisal of their truly valuable work. There can be no doubt of their finding that delinquency, for example, is importantly connected with broken homes, with mental defect, with slums, poverty and other economic factors, and more; and that delinquency often leads straight to adult crime. These and endless other studies in every one of the areas of violence reveal much that is indispensable for our full understanding of the region.

But this is not the only way, not the only fruitful way. Medicine, to illustrate what is here meant, has gained greatly by discovering that several disorders having different names, and affecting different parts of the body—here a visible ulcer, elsewhere a deep pain, or a loss of function—medicine has gained richly by finding that all these are but the varying manifestations of one and the same cause, namely, the invasion of the body by a microscopic organism. The several disorders, until then explained and treated differently, have now received a single explanation and a single mode of therapy. Both understanding and the healing art were advanced by the discovery.

A like gain would come in the understanding and treatment of the varieties of public disorder we are considering, were we to find an underlying and common cause of them all. But the value of such a discovery must not tempt us to see what is not in the evidence itself. The facts must be examined as impartially as possible, to decide the truth or the untruth of what has been suggested. Any examination of the facts that obeys the rules of science must take tested and tried precautions against self-deceit in the examiner.

III

For the purpose just described we should now have before our minds the chief areas of our people's behaviour wherein violence is *frequent*; and immediately following we shall similarly have before us the chief areas wherein violence is *infrequent*, where peace is fairly well established. And the careful reader may then

AN EXPEDITION AND ITS OUTCOME 97

judge for himself as to the truth of any proposed explanation of the far greater amount of violence in the first of these arrays than in the second.

Violence is frequent, in our own country for illustration, in the following areas of behaviour.

1. In all healthy infants, and children until they are well into early youth.
2. In a minority of boys and girls who have reached later youth, and are known as problem youths or delinquents.
3. In a minority of our adults known as criminals—thieves, hold-up men, gangsters, and more.
4. In some employers and employed men, but only in their mutual relations, and not in their relations with other persons.
5. In some persons of the White race and of the Coloured races —mostly rowdies, toughs and the like—in their dealings across the colour-line, and not with those of their own race.
6. In a changing number of persons, usually a small minority, passionately opposed to some policy of government, who join in armed resistance to it, in rioting or rebellion against it.

In all these areas violence is frequent.

Violence is infrequent, peace is established we may say, in the following areas in our nation. The description of these areas may easily seem identical with those just mentioned. A careful reading, however, will show that in no instance is this true.

1. In no healthy infant, and in very few older children until they are well along in their early youth.
2. In the great majority of our boys and girls when they have reached their late youth; they are known as normal youngsters, as well-behaved.
3. In nearly all our adults known as good citizens—farmers, housewives, insurance agents, teachers, doctors, and a long list of others.
4. In many employers and those they employ, in the relations with each other, as well as with men outside this relation with them.

5. In many or most persons of the White race and of the Coloured races, in their relations across the line of colour, and not only with those of their own race.
6. In the very many—usually the overwhelming majority—of our population, toward their government; even when in bitter opposition, theirs is loyal opposition; they vote against rather than shoot those in power.

Now some may at once say that human nature is the cause we seek; for it is of necessity present in all violence, whether by little children or thieves, or in labour disputes, racial riots, or those States that wished to secede from the Union. But human nature is no less present whenever human beings act amicably toward other human beings. Of itself, and until those who offer it in explanation point out what causes it to be violent here, and non-violent there, it does not solve our problem.

Nor is there a clear and consistent economic contrast—of poor and rich, of under-privileged and over-privileged—between the human beings who resort to violence and those who are peaceable. The delinquents and the criminal, it is true, are largely from among the poor; but so also among the poor are millions of our population who are not delinquents, not criminals. And the children, and the youths in their early years, who push and pull, who slap and grab, are not, all of them, the children of the dollar-less, while such children are quite unknown in the homes of bejewelled mothers and coupon-cutting fathers. No, each of the areas of frequent violence does not clearly differ economically from the corresponding area of pacific conduct. The one cause of intentional injury by force is not found in the difference in possessions. The cause lies deeper. For while some are ready to get these goods by force, if need be, others will have them by peaceful and lawful means or go without them forever.

IV

Is there, then, anything of importance which actually is present in each of the six areas of the one array, and absent or markedly weaker in each of the six areas of the opposite array? For only thus can it be acceptable for our election as the cause of the

AN EXPEDITION AND ITS OUTCOME

frequency of violence in the one region and its infrequency in the other.

I believe that here the reader may assure himself that there is a complex of forces, and that the forces found are psychical forces which span the distance between man and man and bring with them the sense that they are members of one body in which human beings, for all their diversity of endowment, and education, and for all their cross-purposes, yet care for one another's life and limb and decencies; and work together in mind and muscle for goods both material and immaterial.

If we run our eyes through the first array do we not find in each of these areas of frequent violence that the human attachments are notably defective? Between the people of our South and the people of our North, the ties of community were not of the strongest even in colonial days; and after the political union of the two sections, these ties were weakened by many decades of increasingly bitter differences about slavery and a State's rights in regard to it, until each feared and distrusted the other, and no lasting pacific settlement could be reached. Mutual understanding had come to an end; then came the shot on Sumter.

Likewise, between the employers and the men they employ, the ordinary fellow-feeling and good-will which most of these men manifest in other areas of their conduct are blighted. The employers generally act like men, with friendly sympathy and a helping hand toward other employers, other business men generally, other citizens. Most of them are generous in their families, toward their golf-mates or fellow club-members. But toward men organized for shorter hours and higher pay, recognition of their union and the closed shop; when they look in this one direction—with some, not all—steel comes into their eyes. What elsewhere is warmth of manner is now chilled. Their jaws close. The men they now have in mind seem as men of an alien race.

And the employed men have like fellow-feeling, generosities and appreciation for men employed; they know what they and their families endure, know their readiness to help when there is need; know their fidelity at the factory in wartime; have only a wise-crack for many a human weakness in all but the one area. But when they speak of managers and those who support them, acid comes into their words—not with all hired men but with many or most. In this one direction bonds of human fellowship are cut as by a linesman, and instead there is antagonism, a conviction that nothing speaks in that direction but hard compulsion. In any area where self-interest is untinctured with fellow-feeling, violence stands ready. It does in fact often win what is not won by appeal to justice.

So it is also where crowd confronts crowd, Whites facing Negroes, not in the South only; White facing Japanese to-day in our Pacific Coast States; or facing Chinese the day before yesterday. The milk of human kindness here curdles. 'We' and 'our' do not cross the racial gulf. The complex social ties which run amongst White Americans even though they know nothing of one another save that they are White and American, here go no farther. The violence is here the companion of alienation, of existence apart, without obligations to one another.

So is it, too, in the criminal toward the bank whose safe he cracks, toward the man for whom he lies in wait. The criminal is not without warm ties—with his pal who has not yet double-crossed him, with some woman, or some child perhaps. But beyond this narrow circle he may have no ties; but only his antagonism, only opportunities for his skill to take.

Delinquent youths also have but few attachments, and these within a narrow circle. Their small gang of companions who likewise are socially detached—only to these are they bound; only to their praise and blame are they sensitive. What is thought of each of them in his own family, or school, by strangers or town is as nothing; he is indifferent whether these commend or condemn.

And—although in less measure—it is so with many younger youths not called delinquents, who fight with one another and take forbidden fruit. They are, it is true, attached to many a person near-by—in family, among playmates, at school and among relatives and the family's friends. But these ties are not strong against a gust of anger or the impulse to have one's way.

Even weaker, more brittle, and extending to fewer persons, are the social attachments of the little child, the infant. The babe knows none at first, but soon shows tenuous ties with one who brings food and fondling and tender care. And in time a little sister may be smiled on, and reached out for, until a small circle is accepted by the babe. But the place of even the accepted one is insecure; some slight opposition to the babe's tiny will may cause him to be cast into outer darkness. Beyond this miniature home-land are only strangers, curious or fearful aliens. The family dog is worth a thousandfold more than all these strangers put together.

To some this evidence may seem enough, and they will say, why labour a now obvious truth. We are persuaded, they may say, that weak social ties, few social ties, social ties of no more than ten yards length, are the invariable accompaniments of self-assertive violence. This proves the case.

But this would not be the way of understanding. It is the way by which men accept as proven what is the cause of crime—now one thing and now another, until perhaps a dozen things are advocated, each as the cause or the chief factor in the cause of crime. They are too-soon convinced; they do not stop to ask : ' But is this pet fact of mine not only present always where crime is present, but always absent where crime is absent? ' For if this is not the case, what we seek is not yet found.

In our present case, then, we must look at each of the areas within which there is little or no violence to see whether the ties of community run unmistakably stronger than where violence often occurs.

The reader, I feel sure, will hardly, after thoughtful looking, fail to find this true. Compare the psychic strands between bodies of men—economic, political, or social—which do not attack with blows and missiles each other's buildings, or members or servants, with those which on occasions do so act. The manufacturer may hate the banker who refused him a loan, but he rarely feels quite ready to throw rocks through the bank's windows, or crack the banker's head as he goes home at dusk. And his restraint is not for love of the banker, but from respect for his own conscience, and for his family. He'd shrivel in his own eyes and in the eyes of others; the thought of violence hardly for even a moment of gentle humour shows its head in his conscious mind.

And, changing the words that need to be changed, this could be said of two crowds, two individuals, both of them white, both negro, both Chinese, both Japanese, anywhere in the United States; each accepts the other as unstrange, unalien; no bitterness is on the tongue, no clenched fist, no ugly set of the jaw. And with most youths nearing manhood, ties grow in strength within a widening round of boys and girls, men and women; and also strengthen within them respect for their community, for law and morals.

This truth may be seen in even greater significance after we have traversed the wide waste of international violence, for which many may long have been eager.

THE TERRAIN OF WAR AND PEACE

I

A traveller of foresight, and especially an explorer, will wish to have at least a general idea of the region he intends to reach and carefully study. And so for ourselves the region now to be explored is in an area among the nations which many will at once say does not exist—an area within which no international war has been waged for a century or more. And just as we say that peace has been established in the United States now for eighty years, although we have been at war several times with foreign powers, so we may say of the region we are about to explore, peace is established in it longer than in our own land since its Civil War, although wars have raged about it. We shall at first see a small area or two which clearly answers to the description, and then prowl about, to decide whether the territory of established peace may not be wider than we expected.

II

The relations between Great Britain and the United States—for all the hard feelings and hot words over the boundary between

Canada and our own country; our fishing rights; over the Confederate privateers from British ports that preyed on Northern shipping in the Civil War—have been pacific since the war of 1812. And this is true, although each of them has repeatedly been at war with other nations, and the United States had a bitter war within its own borders.

In like manner, and not without anger now and then, Denmark, Norway, and Sweden, once given to fierce wars with each other and with nations beyond, have for well over a century lived in mutual peace.

And further, no nation of either of the two groups—the Scandinavian and the English-speaking—has been at war with any nation of the other group. Thus there has been a long avoidance of war, although not of serious disputes, within a circle of five nations, to which France may at once be added, to make a group of six nations mutually pacific throughout the last hundred years or more, three of them Great Powers, and three of them great in much else than the ability to achieve what they desire by force.

But we need not stop here. For nation after nation may be added to this circle, each one of them having had no war with any of the circle's members throughout the latest one hundred years, until the great company—omitting many a lesser sovereignty—includes no less than nineteen states. The names should stand before us—nations that, independent all the while, and not without clashes of interest and aim and not without even armed interventions short of actual war, have managed to maintain peace with one another through a full century or more. They are:

European: Belgium, Denmark, France, Great Britain, the Netherlands, Norway and Sweden in union and then separate, Portugal, Switzerland;

American: Argentina, Bolivia, Brazil, Colombia, Ecuador, Guatemala, Mexico, the United States, Uruguay, Venezuela.

These nations we may call the Mutually Pacific Group.

Now to be compared and contrasted with these nations is a group of states likewise independent throughout the same hundred years which have at some time been at war with one or more of the states just named, and also in this period have been at war with one or more of their own number.

Again omitting some of the lesser sovereignties, the members of the group are:

European: Austria and Hungary in union and then separate, Prussia and then Germany, Piedmont and then Italy, Russia, Spain, Turkey;
American: Chile, Honduras, Nicaragua, Peru;
Asiatic: China, Japan.

We may call these nations the Mutually Belligerent Group.

A comparison of these two groups should lead us far toward a sane appraisal of many an assured assertion, whether by specialists or by plain men, about the forces that produce wars or prevent wars in this troubled world of ours.

III

Let us then begin the exciting search for the cause of the persisting warless inter-relations within our 'Mutually Pacific Group' in a world ravaged and rent by war. And first we should pay heed to a goodly number of the prominent explanations of war and peace already before us in an earlier chapter and at once to be named again. If a particular explanation is correct, what it declares to be the cause of war should be more powerfully present in the more belligerent group of nations than in the circle of nations among which mutual warfare has been avoided for a century or more. But if, on the contrary, the proposed 'cause' of war is equally present in both of the groups of nations or is, if anything, more powerfully present among the pacific than among the belligerent group, then we may forthwith reject the proposed explanation as quite unsupported by the evidence, and we must seek an explanation that fits the facts. The far-from-complete array of these 'causes', each of which is held by its particular believers to be *the* cause of war, should now be tried on this touch-stone to see if it is genuine.

Human nature, the instinct of pugnacity, the unconscious or subconscious, and 'mass psychology' may all be considered together; for most of what should be said of any one of the four must be said of the others as well.

Each of them, so far as we yet know, is present and active in every human being. It is a part or manifestation of his natural endowment, and is at the base of all he does, in his particular physical and social environment, whatever be his race, religion, habitat, or nationality. Each nation, in both our groups alike, then, we have no good reason to doubt, has a fair allotment of human nature, of pugnacity, of unconscious or subconscious energies, and of whatever is true in 'mass psychology'. Each of the facts named in these explanations as the cause of war is an indubitable and dynamic fact. But since each such fact is found in every nation of our Mutually Pacific Group and yet is no more present in every nation of the belligerent group, it cannot explain the striking difference in the mutual behaviour—here pacific, there belligerent—of the two groups. None of these 'causes', nor the whole of them together, is the answer to our inquiry.

IV

Thus dissatisfied with these examples of current psychological proposals, we may turn to a few of another type. And let us look first at the belief that *Capitalism* is the source of war, and that until the world is rid of it there can be no peace.

Our two groups of nations, however, disturb one's confidence in this account. For in the Mutually Pacific Group are the chief capitalist nations of the world—the United States and Great Britain. And with them, and at peace with them are many nations in some of which Capitalism has held an important place, while in others it is weak. Comparing with these mutually pacific nations the group which has been mutually belligerent do we find that Capitalism plays among them a still more important role? For this should be the case were Capitalism the cause of war. But we find the very opposite to be true. Capitalism is *less* powerful in these nations and more powerful in the more pacific group. The century of mutual peace in this circle, then, cannot be accounted for by an absence or weakening of the capitalist system.

So of Capitalism; and now of unequal pressures of population, supposed by not a few important persons to be the cause of war. Countries of denser population, these believe, must war upon nations of less dense population to sustain the very life of their own people. But what is here to follow will but slay the slain, for Carr-Saunders has given this belief its death blow. For in our Mutually Pacific Group there is such a difference of pressure between Great Britain and the United States; between Belgium, or Holland—countries of high pressure—and any of the Latin-American countries, in all of which the pressure is low. Peace in the circle cannot be explained by a virtual equality of such pressure among its member-nations.

And in the belligerent group Germany has been ready to wage war upon countries like Belgium of denser population than herself; and Russia has not conquered region after region because of her own dense population. Further, India and China, countries with exceedingly dense populations, have suffered wars from others far more often than they have themselves originated wars.

Nor do we find here a confirmation of the belief so loudly asserted near the beginning of the Second World War, that armed violence between nations is due to the ugly contrasts between '*Haves*' and '*Have-nots*'. If this were true, we should expect to see an equality of national possessions, either by there being in our pacific group no 'Have-nots', or else no 'Haves'. We find nothing of the kind: the United States lives at peace with Mexico, France with Portugal, Great Britain with Denmark. Those of great possessions live in the same world with those who possess little, and no war comes between them.

It is true there has been and there still is a wide disparity in possessions among the nations in our Belligerent Group—between Russia, for example, and every other nation in that group. But the disparities in the Mutually Pacific circle have been and still are no less great.

And the last of these explanations to be tested by the facts is this: that international war arises inevitably because of national sovereignty and a lack of common government over the whole body of nations. Now the present writer earnestly feels the need of world government and must not be understood to be opposing it here. And yet while the Belligerent Group assuredly is without any such international government, this is no less true of the Mutually Pacific Group. Peace, then, according to the explanation we are testing, is impossible until national sovereignty is swept away, and there is the one sure foundation for peace—an international government. And yet here stand before us a great company of fully sovereign nations, both powerful and petty, both rich and poor, that actually have had not a single war amongst them for a full century or more. Now this fact does *not* indicate that these nations are better off with their sovereignty jealously maintained, and any common political rule over them sedulously avoided. What the facts do show is what can be done even with and in spite of sovereignty and wholly without a common government, but where other forces are at work, forces powerful and beneficent, but too little recognized.

V

With so many honoured proposals which *do not* explain the more frequent occurrence of war within the one group of nations, and its entire absence within the other group, we must now press on to discover if possible, what *does* explain this strange contrast.

The peace maintained in the Warless Circle of nations, their restraint from mutual violence, is due to many forces, not all of which can here be considered. But primarily the cause lies in a gradually reduced fear and suspicion of one another; and a gradually acquired hope of benefits from friendly behaviour toward some or many member-nations of this group. Each of these nations, by experience through years, has come to some degree of confidence in the intentions of the others toward itself, confidence in the advantage of keeping its own conduct pacific toward these others. Often misguided and nearly always self-seeking as every nation appears in the eyes of every other nation, yet from this gnarled material has come a co-operation not only against some nations outside the circle, but also—and far oftener—for the welfare of the collaborators; for trade, communications, health and a score of other things valued.

Self-interest is a power in human affairs, but is not the only power. And almost shame-facedly in a large number of the Warless Circle there has arisen some honest appreciation, or respect, some regard for these companions not only as means to one's own separate ends, but as worth helping for their own sake. The feeling in the United States toward Great Britain is coloured with this; as is Britain's regard for France, so important in the civilization which they share. Thus within the Mutually Pacific Group a sense of a common heritage is cherished and enlarged. Mutual sympathy thus comes timidly on the scene to temper the alienation there. It is the beginning of fellowship, of social ties which, when strengthened, transform men hitherto mutually aloof, into a community, wherein they think of themselves and others as 'we', and of the general attainments and perils as 'ours'. Men so bound together prefer the ties, and are unwilling to see them broken. And they prefer to settle their mutual grievances by pacific ways rather than by war-like. Invisible and often unrecognized as are these social ties, they are powerful in most individuals and in many nations to check the natural impulse to have one's will by brute force. The violent way is the unsocial way; and men are basically social. Powerful in men, who begin to care for one another, it drives them to create the instruments of peace, against the instruments of combat; to create government and all its implements to minister to social needs. And even where there is a deep antipathy to any international government, and yet also a deep desire for peace conjoined with strengthening social bonds, peace can be maintained—as in the Mutually Pacific Group we have been considering.

When now we turn to the Belligerent Group, we find little or nothing of those early stages of community so clear in the other circle. Mutual distrust outweighs any mutual confidence.

Germany or Prussia have been increasingly ready to despoil others of their group. And Russia and Turkey; Russia and Japan; Japan and China, have had no reason for friendliness with one another. Nor has Italy, as the century wore on, given Austria or Germany, or Turkey, any confidence that she will be considerate of their interests. Co-operation in peacetime within this Belligerent Group is far more difficult than in the mutually pacific circle. And in these belligerent nations there has not been and is not that consciousness of common political, social and religious ideals, and of belonging together, that is unmistakably found among many of the nations of the circle that has kept the peace within its borders for a century or more. The bellicose group lacks the degree of cohesion, the communal ties that are present within the pacific circle. This complex factor, notably stronger where peace is maintained than where the peace is often broken, meets the test by which science decides the value of any offered explanation. None of the prominent explanations examined earlier could pass this test—neither human nature nor pugnacity, neither 'mob psychology' nor the subconscious. Nor is the test met by capitalism, nor the contrast between 'haves' and 'have-nots'; neither by the pressure of population, nor even by national sovereignty and independence. No one of these is present or absent, is stronger or weaker, in the manner to be expected were it the cause of war or the cause of peace.

Now it is true that social ties, communal ties never act alone; other forces act with them to increase or lessen their powers for peace. And wars arise from more than the mere absence of social or communal ties. Yet the evidence strongly indicates that the presence or absence of these ties is of central importance. And guided by this knowledge the constructive work for world peace can proceed with good hope.

It will not have escaped the reader that the explanation here offered for the presence or absence of violence between nations is virtually the same as the explanation for the presence or absence of violence within the nation. It may now be well to consider this unexpected breadth of the explanation.

THE WORTH OF WHAT WE'VE FOUND

And now, after a rest from traversing such varied domains, we should bring together and appraise what has come of it all. What is at the centre of our findings; how do these stand with respect to the reports of others; and what are our gains both for understanding and for effective effort against the forces so increasingly destructive within the homeland and between nations.

I

The discovery that stands above all else we observed is this. Human violence wherever found and however portentous its character and name—the babe's feeble resistance to control, the youths' delinquency, on through adult crime, the clubbing and throwing of rocks outside the gates of industry, the riots between white and coloured men, and political rebellion, on and out into war-waging by nations—all these are psychically of one pattern, and they issue from one source. They are man's physical effort to down opposition by others to his own desires, and they occur with especial frequency between persons who are not bound together by those ties that run between men who, in very mind and not in name only, are fellow-members of a community.

And we also saw, in contrast, that the many forms of pacific behaviour between men—whether acting singly or in groups, small or large, whether in domestic or international life, and whatever their name—men and women, bricklayers and doctors, crowds, business firms, the staffs of theatres, hospitals, athletic and religious bodies, and even powerfully armed nations—that all these, when the psychical bounds of fellow-feeling and purpose are stronger than their mutual dislike and distrust, live through endless trials and tribulations from one another and yet rarely or never come to blows.

Thus are brought together many forms of human behaviour hitherto commonly regarded as disconnected and each having its own separate cause. They are found to be deeply alike, and to be explained by variation of a powerful factor common to them all. In spite of their diverse appearance, a single formula or law fits them all. This is a justifiable simplification, the discovery of an inclusive common explanation—a kind of result that is highly prized in science. We understand better a far-extended, rich and terrible domain of human conduct.

II

But what of the findings by other workers in one or more of the areas here brought into one? Are their results to be looked on with contempt and brushed aside as worthless?

On the contrary our present account accepts such results as have been scientifically established and gives them a place in the larger whole, although a different place perhaps from that assigned them by some of their eager sponsors. Let me speak of these in large samples; for even a word or two about each of a long procession of the lesser kinds would here be out of place.

The innumerable matters over which men fight—nations over markets, materials, territory, 'life-lines', and more; industrial manager and his men over wages, hours, and the rest; on down to the child that grabs its playmate's toy—such things are said to be the cause of their fighting. They cannot be denied their place, but not a fundamental place. They are the objects of violent struggle only by those who already face each other with antagonism or deep suspicion. Of themselves they are not the cause of fighting. The nations of our warless circle have seen these things in their midst and at most have scowled, clenched their teeth and turned to the day's work. Deep forces within them held them from brawling. To name the things men fight for does not tell us why *here* they fight for them, while *there* such possessions are sought by pacific means or else not at all. Our present study brings an answer to the question left unanswered by naming merely the bones of contention.

Findings of a different kind are likewise not denied or made light of in the present explanation, but would have an honoured though not the highest place. As was said before, there can be no doubt that the crimes of youth and of adults are closely connected with the slum, with ignorance, vice, dangerous drugs, the broken home, and with criminal associates inside and outside of prison. The violence in economic and in racial disputes is probably connected with some of these, although also with special forces besides.

But since in poverty, ignorance, the broken home, and much else, are reared many children who do *not* become burglars, gangsters or murderers, these surroundings are *not* of themselves the prime and sure source of the criminal's manner of behaviour.

In the criminal, the slum and all else of its kind are the frequent companions of the forces which leave him alien to the large fellowship. The strands of this fellowship are foreign to his mind and habit, and he follows instead his own crude promptings.

The present account of violence thus denies nothing that comes of sound research. But in so far as the findings give no heed to the individuals' or the groups' alienation from their society, they are seen to be deeply insufficient.

III

Communal ties are equal to the heavy work ascribed to them in the present account. They have it in them to play a major role in causing the immense difference in the behaviour toward their fellow-men, let us say, of 'Scarface', Al Capone and General Booth, or in the mutual behaviour of Germany and France and that of Great Britain and the United States. We should spend a moment in looking at forces whose weakness or strength result in such contrasts.

The strands that connect men or large bodies of men are living activities in them, as diverse and as subject to change as the living tissues of our muscles and nerves. They consist of our readiness to work with them, this work finding powerful support in fellow-feeling, confidence and in emotions allied with these. It is true there may be divisive activities of every kind, from emotion to intellect and aim; but these are subordinate, overruled, unable to annul the partnership, the co-operation. And this co-operation, both bodily and mental, appeared in a much earlier part of this writing as one of the central energies in the power that reared the pyramids, and piled walls against the savage North. And by these energies the scattered fragments of humanity were united into nations, nation-communities, each with armed might and the still greater might of law expressing the common will. This power resident in each true member restrains his hand and self-will from striking his fellow-member, and instead invites him to join with him in labour for the common weal. The man, the group of men not sharing in this power is without the constraint, the inhibition, and does violence by self-will untinctured by the great aims around him. The ties of community varying as they do in strength and sweep in different persons, and in the same person with change of time and situation—these lines of force are fully able to account for the dramatic conflict between the powers that upbuild and the powers that bring rack and ruin.

IV

The practical value of our new view should not be without accent. For in knowing the deep sources of violence and of peaceful behaviour we can become more and more sure in our treatment, and in the prevention of world war, and domestic violence in its many forms. No less can we act confidently to strengthen and extend the peace already achieved among very many of the nations, and among nearly all the individuals, and nearly all the groups within the borders of our own partially turbulent country, and of other countries as well. There are practical gains of two important kinds that should now be sketched broadly, leaving until later the details.

The first gain for treatment and prevention is in knowing what is at the bottom of the business we would rid ourselves of and would replace by what we long for. This gives us the clue to what must be done, difficult as this may be. For it requires that men be made readier to join with others in creative work on themselves as individuals, and on themselves also as members of bodies, of organizations of men. The social machinery now at work must continue at work, but there will be added the convinced purpose to have minds deeply changed in their connections with one another; readier for mutual respect and its right expression, and readier against gains won by force and the threat of force. It is a great gain that we can gauge and direct our practice for peace and against violence, wherever they appear, and whatever their form. We have no easy cure, but we can create more effective methods; and waste less effort on ways that leave unchanged the springs of the good we would have; and of the bane we would destroy.

V

With this first practical gain thus in mind, a second and even more substantial benefit should be recognized. It is, that the deep therapy here required against violence and for peaceful human relations, can bring in much more than these rich results. The dynamic communal ties that restrain men from using fists and clubs and bombs to attain their ends can be made to act against gaining one's ends by means that are *without violence* yet are as injurious as violence itself, or even more injurious. Noiseless damage—consciously done and speciously justified—is not alone by crass cheating, and lying, but by highest possible profits at the lowest possible wages, or by the highest possible wages and the least possible service; or by mass-production of irresistible superfluities for a society most of whose members are not well nourished, clad, housed, medically attended, and educated; and by nursing in themselves and spreading to others untruths about those who are not of their own class or culture, or those not of their own race or nationality.

These and a myriad other poisons, not detectable by any chemist, are the unviolent means of getting what is desired, regardless, or but too slightly mindful of the common life, of the common good. The man who is alive, every millimetre of him, to the pain, and the satisfaction of his fellows and of his city, and his nation, cannot easily have his will at such cost. The same communal interlacings which hold him from setting fire to his neighbour's house, or stabbing him, can be made to check any stirrings of intention to get what he wants by subtle but legally allowable means. Such means injure men's faith in one another and lessen their readiness to labour in concert for the good life of all.

What was found by our search into violence and into peaceful conduct is thus of high value, making us sure, intelligently sure of this course against the black shame within every nation and between nations. Our shame can be wiped out by men with powers to produce goods a millionfold beyond all the wonders of Aladdin's lamp now united to turn their creative powers to this other work. But we should seek further insight into the ways and means to our goal, and to down doubts and give us courage.

VII

THE WILDS AND THEIR RECLAMATION

MEN'S NATURE WHEN UNRECLAIMED

WE have long had before us some of the many forms of violence, from the puny rebellion of babes to the armed aggression of empires. Forces deep in men's structure contend with other forces no less deep. And the whole struggle may well be thought distantly as though our human spirits were enacting an early scene of Milton's great drama, in which the ministers of Creative Wisdom are struggling to defeat the rebellious among them and hurl them headlong to a nine-days' fall.

In our mundane conflict we have seen some of the main sources of the destructive power, whose latest outburst has spread ruin across continents and confusion throughout the world. And the disclosure of these sources has suggested the work that to-day and for years to come must claim a first rank of urgency—the work of extending and strengthening those psychical connections that make for peace and more than peace. It is a labour exceeding anything imposed on Hercules. But mere difficulty will not daunt men who create like gods. What will daunt multitudes of men is the belief that the task of fulfilment is contrary to the very nature of things, is impossible because of ineradicable drives in man's inherited constitution. If this be true, we should know it, accept it, and not waste our effort on anything Quixotic. Let us turn then to human nature, what it is and whether it makes idle the great enterprise here proposed.

I

Once upon a time, so runs the well-known folk-tale, there was a courtier named Valentine, a man of gentle birth, and of valour. And there came to the court repeated rumours of a wild man who held the whole countryside in dread. He was shaggy, of powerful frame, and so fierce that few dared meet, and none had ever vanquished him. So Valentine went forth with brave companions, fully armed; and after much adventure came upon the wild man, Orson, and in single combat defeated him. And then, amazed, he found that Orson was his very brother who, lost since a babe, nurtured by a bear, had grown to manhood to be the terror of all that region.

This story would rightly to-day be counted an entertaining absurdity; such a contrast between brothers cannot be produced by a mere difference in their nurture. And yet the tale may do for us what was not intended. Valentine and Orson may stand for what two opposed schools teach of man as he really is by his natural inheritance, of man untouched as yet by circumstances —by 'the slings and arrows of outrageous fortune' or by the gentling of a happier lot. Which of the two presentments, Valentine or Orson, comes nearer to the truth? Or does each of them tell a truth, a half-truth about us? A just answer will weigh heavily for or against the work mankind now faces.

II

In what direction should we seek the answer to this vital question? Not by observing grown men and women in New York, Laramie, nor even in Papua; in these persons we never find pure nature, but nature overcast and intermingled with private learning and social usage. No; we must instead go to very young children, and later to animals. Only thereafter may we look to adults.

The behaviour of little children awakens serious doubt of the oft-repeated account of natural man as a creature wholly contentious, predatory, acquisitive, lustful, egoistic and self-willed. The young child, it is true, when he gains strength and free movement strikes out, and struggles against what at the moment he dislikes—being laid down, or picked up, or clothed or fed. He cries, grabs and holds fast what he desires. And when older and at play snatches from others, slaps, scratches, pulls hair, for his purpose. Without having learned it, he falls down, kicks the floor, and screams when thwarted by the Great Powers, and soon—nature now supplemented by shrewd observation—uses the nuisance value, or learns the futility of such explosions. But blacken his character as the facts may, other facts declare him also to be the very opposite of the little tyrant of this account, for his acts no less loudly declare him upon many an occasion to be forgetful of self, interested in other little children; at first in naked curiosity he watches them, but soon is showing his uncalculating pleasure in being with them. At play with another child on the floor, the two are not always quarrelling. They may co-operate in building or in tearing down; one may freely offer some toy to the other. And the child weeps and wails when his playmate is taken away from the common enterprise.

The facts themselves here speak for many contrasting motives in early conduct, and speak against the simplicities of the realist's dogma. The child is as really—although perhaps less strikingly—urged on by an uncalculating liking for others, especially other playmates, and by an in-born readiness for joining with others in action.

These forms of companionship are real and as natural as are their very opposites—the readiness to exclude others, to resist them, and to show them anger and dislike. The child has both of these modes of conduct deep in his native constitution. Some of the learned ascribe to his natural endowment those traits and only those traits society condemns; for them Orson is the true child of human nature. Others would have us believe that the child is endowed only with what is admirable; Valentine is for them nature's child. But actually the truth, so the facts aver, is in neither of these views alone, but in both when rightly purged and combined.

And this conclusion with regard to children is in complete accord with the findings of specialists in the study of animals.

III

Men, we may well conclude then, are endowed with powers and impulses to act in varied and even in opposing ways—to move about and to lie still and sleep; to observe and to imagine; to remember and forget.

It should be understood, however, that individuals differ from one another in their psychical endowment, even as they do physically; one person abler for training in mathematics; another, in music; still another in the command of others; and so on. Yet despite all this, there are features of mind that are by nature common to all men. He has it in him to feel sympathy and antipathy, to love, to fear and to hate. He can hope and he can despair; he can build and he can destroy. He is able to act alone and to act with others. He can be busy without aim, or be afire with purpose. And with all, and nearly the greatest of these powers, is the power to learn—that is, not only the power to acquire new skill, new knowledge, new understanding, but also to acquire new purposes, new interests, new objects for one's desire and attachment, one's love and fear and abhorrence.

Thus the powers with which the individual is endowed can be modified in his own life-time; they can be educated, and fitted for new modes of life—from sleeping to eating, from curiosity to sex, from domination to sympathy and friendliness. Human society and civilization depend on this plasticity of men's natural gifts.

Thus we have gained an answer to the oft-debated question whether human nature can be changed—the answer is: 'Yes, it can be deeply changed, and is changed in nearly every person who has passed from infancy to adult membership in any human community.

And yet the very opposite answer must also be given. For in all the eventful years between birth and maturity the main pattern of the man's endowment has not been changed; he is still a person able and desiring to eat, sleep, imagine, have companionship, and so on indefinitely. It is as with the human face, that alters profoundly between birth and old age, and yet retains all the while its muscular and boney structure in which are eyes, nose, lips, forehead and chin. Human nature is unchangeable, yet changes ceaselessly.

These are among the richly varied gifts for man's use.

But the full tale of our inheritance is not told until there is recounted what is not given us, what is withheld. And must be acquired, if at all, by experience and by our own effort and also by the help of others. We are as heirs of a wise benefactor who knows when to withhold, knows what *not* to give to those of high destiny. Men are not treated as are some of the animals— the solitary wasps, for instance, whose female's action is prescribed by her inherited constitution in unbelievable detail. She prepares a concealed place for her young; and, for their food, she stores it with living creatures she has paralysed; closes the nest and leaves them untended, uninstructed as she has been left.

In contrast to this marvel of fore-ordination, immense areas of human endowment come unfinished, unmapped out, for us to deal with for ourselves. Our native power to imagine comes to us empty, for us to fill. Our native power to think leaves one man free to think of wheat fields and ploughing, and another, of law and justice. Our native readiness to fight does not prescribe what we shall fight about, or when, against whom, or with what means. And so it is with our inherited impulses to fear, to acquire property, to be friendly, to mate, and a score of other types of activity. Nature hands us over to ourselves and others, unfinished, not even half-finished.

But this is not yet the full story of our natural incompleteness. Our impulsions or 'drives' are ill-proportioned to one another; self-interest, for instance, being far more insistent, more overbearing than interest in others, which begins hesitant and is easily overborne.

And still further of our incompleteness, our powers, by nature alone, are largely in a state of anarchy, or are under only fitful control. Only in the course of life, the person himself having a voice in the matter, may some manner of government be established. Perhaps the impulse to possess comes to control all else in the man, imagination, curiosity, sex, friendliness, and his desire to master others. And the man eventually may stand forth, perhaps the richest on a continent; or perhaps a notorious highwayman, or a close-fisted small trader. Nature alone does not decide whether cupidity or sex or any other of our drives shall be master, and whether it will, while master, be tempered by other powers.

The man is brought forth into this world with none of these pre-determined, as to the integration of his native powers. The little child shows itself this ungoverned, unintegrated person, with ready tears and laughter, curious about everything, now grasping, now giving, now all affection and then all protest and self-will. This is but a glimpse of humanity in the rough, as nature passes it over to us—human powers without skill and understanding and ungoverned within; ready for all manner of inner uprising or tyranny.

V

As was said earlier, the man we see in ourselves and others is an artifact, made largely by human art from crude natural substance—to compare great with small—as the Indian's spear-head is shaped from flint. And, stripping away what is done to a man in the course of his life, by his physical surroundings, his own workmanship and that of his human associates, we have caught sight of what he was originally, what the crude natural stuff of him is. We found it wonderful beyond all common imagining, and yet a full life's journey distant from even the half of the promise in him.

Man, it may now appear true, is by nature generously, indeed lavishly endowed with abilities, promptings and powers; multitudinous, complementary, and conflicting. He receives them unskilled, undisciplined, ungoverned, ready for any use and purpose that gains mastery over them. He is ready to be made into one who cheats and stabs, or one who cleanses and heals, and builds. By nature he is the most richly provided and the most fragmentary, the least finished of all the many wonders of the world. Almost by his natural endowment alone he can live and mature, and as the wind blows, he mates, fondles or abandons; he takes or throws to others, or crushes what he holds. He is as a waste land with wild flowers and prickly pears, fair to the artist's eye, but deadly for habitation, until re-claimed by ditches and the plow.

AIMS OF THE RECLAMATION

I

The human wasteland, arid and untilled, is ready to yield an overflowing harvest if given the needed care. Without that care man is unendurable to most of his fellow-men, and cannot participate in the life of the community.

And now from what we know of this nature of ours, and from what has already come from our rich endowment, there are clear signs of much that begs to be changed, and for which we may reasonably labour at once and in the near and distant future.

In the meagrest sketch, the needed work is to invite and spur every person to set his powers to live as much more than an animal as he can; to create as becomes his human endowment, and to accept and make his own what we earlier have seen to be indispensable for the creative use of his native abilities.

Each person, it is true, is unique, and his reclamation must heed this; yet all persons have many needs in common and some of these now may well be brought to mind.

Negatively there is the need of riddance of many forms of activity, inner and outer, that later may be serious barriers between the man and his own purposes, and his fellow-working with others—a matter that finally becomes habitual and effortless.

Decent living to-day, and not a detached ideal, demands this of us. For, as the evidence has indicated, delinquency, crime, international war, and all their horrible kindred alike, come forth when communal ties are absent or at their weakest, leaving men free to seize and hold, to hate, strike, and kill, according to their crude natural impulses. Democracy in particular, with its necessary faith in plain men, has a vain faith if their faith is in plain men who have been unreclaimed. And those who would be creators of literature, painting, and musical composition at a high level, miss their mark if they believe that their natural gifts, untouched by the community, can be made their sole reliance. They, of all men, stand in need of the transformation. Our day especially, and our own country suffers from want of this transformation and from disbelief in it.

Positively there is required for every man, be he genius or not, a thousand forms of activity, inner and outer, that in time will be counted by the man himself and by others as among his surest means of achievement. Nature alone gives no such activities. They must be acquired, if the person is not to live amid needless and invisible barriers.

II

These general aims of reclamation may now be brought to clearer focus, to bring out details that cannot be ignored without loss to the work.

Every chief power in our lavish endowment—to perceive, to speak, to remember and imagine, to think and understand, to care for one's self and to become attached to others; to enjoy, love, fear and hate; and to purpose and act in connection with all these activities of ours and many more—these must be brought to do their fitting work. Each of these powers can do immeasurably better than it does by bare nature. And above all else is the man's stature decided by the objects to which he becomes attached, around which his intelligence plays, and in whose service his purposes go forth in ceaseless energy. What comes of a man's natural endowment is decided largely by what he comes to love, think about and to which he gives his will.

Regarding these fateful attachments, and our service to their objects—food or sport, and all else up to the highest—they are not activities of pure intellect. But men are misled to-day who regard them as *emotions*. Instead our emotions serve these, but are as different from the affections themselves as is the retainer from his high lord. These forces, higher than the emotions, steady the magnetic currents that hold the needle to the north and the pilot to his course. The Monk Mendel at his quest with his peas; the man of integrity holding to his principles; the fearful soldier standing steadfast at his post of duty in the dark; Grenfell drifting on his ice pan calm and unafraid under a higher will—these attachments are not gifts of nature but have been made out of natural acts into sterner stuff than gusts of passionate anger or fear; they are like the heart that awaits no momentary excitement, but pulses on, day and night, year by year. Human reclamation must look to men's attachments or no man will be reclaimed. The attachments with the understanding are the main stuff of the conscious purposive life, the will of man. The attachments will be among the objects of prime concern.

The care for attachments and the purposed effort will aim to have men hold to objects suited to man's pre-eminence, to his power to create. And the utmost will be done to have each man establish in himself and others a threefold object to be prized, protected, and made still worthier of his esteem—to become, indeed, bone of his bone.

The first part of this triple attachment is the person's concern for himself as a man, distinct, endowed for rare accomplishment. Another part of this triple attachment is his concern for his fellow-men as individuals, each of whom is likewise endowed for rare accomplishment. The final part of this threefold object is the community of himself and his fellow-men to which each individual is largely indebted for whatever degree of fulfilment his inborn powers have yet attained. And this object of attachment must become enlarged to be the Great Community unlimited by name or sign, by time or place. This rounded object of one's attachment and will is the necessary corrective of all those 'isms'—communism, fascism, nationalism, and others that infest our day.

Each of these 'isms' is an unbalanced zeal for a part—but only a part—of the entire object that calls for our attachment and purpose. And the zealot is so forgetful or contemptuous of all but his beloved fragment of the good, that he is ready savagely to mutilate all other parts of it. Hitler would wreck many a nation for the sake of Germany; the Japanese Military for the sake of Japan; and the Russian communists for Russia and the workers' class. And not wholly dissimilar is the blinding attachment of many a person to the White race, or some Coloured race; to the individual, or to some social system; to art or science; or to the advance of some one or other partial good to the neglect or ruin of all else.

The aim of reclamation will be to complete rather than destroy these partial attachments and purposes. It must correct its own shortcomings; for its effect on any individual or group is commonly far from complete, and what there is of it may be lessened by silent corrosion, or almost swept away by mass enthusiasm.

III

By nature men are overweighted with some animal desires, and underweighted with those distinctively human. Reclamation would fall far short if it took our powers indiscriminately and gave to each of them new strength and skill. In general, our natural supply of anger and pugnacity, well suited to an almost animal existence, are more than enough for the good life of peaceable men. And our impulses of sex come so early and are so insistent as often to obstruct or halt the preparation and masterwork of rare ability. Reclamation will be directed to correct this disproportion—this unbalance. And an equal disproportion, though of opposite direction, must be corrected: desires, sensitivities, impulses too weak must be brought to power, to authority. The timid weakling of the play-ground must be brought forward; the bully held back.

Self-regard, indispensable though it is, is nature's eminent trouble-maker. Its corrective is man's natural interest in others, his readiness for companionship; for lending a hand where a hand is called for. This side of our nature, so over-shadowed by human self-interest that many cannot see it at all, must be brought out, given confidence in its office and future, and trained to its best work. Without it seated high in the council, no individual, no nation comes into its own. Your giant egoists, your Hitlers, are sure of their bad eminence in our annals. They are monstrosities among the unreclaimed like the sabre-toothed tigers of our asphalt pits. Self-regard unbalanced by regard for others is the bane of our economic life. It distorts politics. It obstructs justice. It embitters the intercourse between nations and between races. Unbalanced self-regard is the fountain-head of violence and all its fellow evils; it is the enemy of those connections of men with men that are the primal substance of the community; and indirectly it renders impossible such creative work as is most honoured.

But reclamation will aim at more than a counter-balancing of our native desires and impulses. The aim is also to enlarge and complete the work of each, not to annul it. Selling ruled by self-interest and also by interest in the welfare of the buyer would be the aim. And for pugnacity there would be sought not its counter-balance by submission, but by having over both of these a concern for the common good, with eagerness for the good fight.

And all our native impulses and desires would be linked with the native curiosity heightened to understanding. To make our impulse to possess, and our impulse to bestow, and all the rest of our native powers act in the light of the fullest possible insight —this must be our goal. For no man may be said to have come forth from the wilds until all these abilities acquaint themselves with one another and put their hands unitedly to the work.

IV

These many powers within us need a befitting control, or government. Nature does not give us minds well-governed; this control which we need comes only by artifice, by design, the result of the re-making of men.

The young child's will is the weather-vane's will; if no better control is artfully established, it will be little more than the will of the animal, driven now by hunger, now by sex, again by private pugnacity or the solidarity of the herd. Inner government is essential for the production that is crowned with highest honour. It is needed by the man of exceptional talent, but also by the plain man as well, he, too, with his priceless heritage waiting to be fashioned into excellence. His mind must not only be made whole, integrated, but so organized that the forces for a good life have command, ruling the unruly desires or 'drives', yet giving them their place. A unity such as this enlarges each power, and sacrifices none. The extreme specialist, whether in art, politics, or science, misses this result, to his own regret, as did Darwin.

A nation, a civilization that encourages and even urges its men of great talent to this narrowing course is itself astray. It buys its rareties at a needlessly high price. Men of good-will would prefer a re-making of men that would be as intent on minds of fair proportions as ever were the Greeks on grace of body.

V

There is need and there must be ceaseless care that the self-government within the mind be not despotic, intolerant of inner opposition and criticism. There must be an honoured place for the mentor, the censor that passes judgment, especially on one's purposes and deeds. It advises, it endorses, it prohibits. Socrates knew it and gave it honour. And indeed its presence is among our salient possessions, for the highest of living things in our world, other than men, are without it; it marks us from the beasts. Yet it has its own defects; it, too, needs to be reclaimed. The work of making men into what is promised in them, must include discovery of ways to add wisdom to the inner judge's wisdom, and to give its decisions weight for the man's own will. In centuries to come, it may well appear that here more and more is one of many points at which the person is in contact with what exceeds him, and is encouraged to go beyond what is the ruling passion of his people and the spirit of his time.

VI

The community itself also needs reclaiming, needs persons made new to goad and instruct their society to attain a higher level.

Beyond the solitary governed mind is the concert of governed minds, where the thoughts and purposes of many conspire. This is far from a counsel of perfection. It is but to require of ourselves that we carry to a higher pitch in old fields and extend into new a work long in progress and visible in present times.

There is, for example, an increasing solicitude for the unwillingly unemployed, and the unemployable, for the sick and the aged, for those maimed in industry. The time is past when for many the broken soldier stood almost alone among plain men in receipt of such compassion. With free public education for every child and youth, and the increasing rights and fuller opportunities for women, along with all other indications of the enlargement of spirit recounted in earlier chapters of this writing, there is solid ground for confidence that men can and must take in hand their biological and cultural heritage and shape it still further toward what will satisfy and delight.

THE WAYS OF THE DYNAMIC PROCESS

The transforming of natural human beings into members of a community is far from what those believe who think it is a matter wholly of compulsion. Man is no piece of steel to be pressed exactly into shape and made part of a machine. He assumes his new form not without pressures and blows, it is true, but more by incitements and invitation, to add here, to subtract there of himself. Infinite is the variety of these inducements, and their continuance is through years. The activities that reclaim his mind and body are a conjunction of forces both from within and from without, from his own unique constitution and from his own unique surroundings, especially his human surroundings. Each person selects from what is offered him by others. He prefers some kinds of change in him, and joins with outer forces in their direction; other changes he will have none of, and the influences favouring them find him adamant.

The process will be found to have much in common with that of bringing special talents to fruition, described earlier. But now our eyes are intent, not on rare ability, but on the powers possessed by almost all men—Newton and the bus-driver alike, and on the organization of these powers for good, plain human living.

I

The dynamic process here called reclamation begins in the home with the mother's encouragement of the babe's suitable acts in eating, grasping and sleeping, or of those acts that are delightful to her—his smile, laughter, and happy gurgling, or his free movements of head, arms and legs. And in time small self-controls are brought to pass, as befits one destined to wear the toga. The wished-for behaviour is led on into habit by endearments or varied signs of disapproval shown by the mother and others of the household, and later by the praise and silent wonder of visitors, and the unpremeditated art of playmates. Thus he learns the beggarly elements of conduct, and finds that his own satisfactions and privations are part and parcel of his heed or disregard of the feelings and desires not of himself alone, if he is to enjoy companions and games instead of ostracism from the romp, the fray, the swimming. The rough handling of him by older brothers and sisters may be worth more than crown jewels. He learns the code of youth—not to hit a fellow when down, not to hit below the belt, not to blab, lie or steal—good restrictions on the child of nature, like most of the Ten Commandments, and not a bad underpinning for more constructive morals then and later. By many a reward and punishment, some of them as soft as sealskin, others of grit, the youth comes to behave somewhat acceptably, and also comes to prefer such behaviour in himself and in others; and he joins in bestowing reward and punishment on his fellows. Children and youths, for all their Bolshevist impulses, are also Tories; they hold to the established order, to the good old ways which were quite new to them a year ago.

And there is the power of wise and gentle ridicule. Redskins, it is said, made ridicule the mainstay in the education of the boy; the elders deriding the youngster who breaks down at a test by fire or violates some rule of conduct. Ridicule is also effective among our own sanctions, from youth on in creating man's very fibre.

And in this earlier period comes schooling, in which, on playground and in class, most of the forces just named—praise, ridicule and all the rest—work mightily along with knowledge that comes of the round earth and the men on it; of their life now and through the centuries, of their achievements, good and evil, their aspirations and intentions. Some—Adams, Sitwell and others of their schooling—make moaning literature of the whole business; but in the end the plain lad and lass find their urns brimming, and they press on with light step along ways as old as humanity and also along ways never trod before.

II

When youth is passing, the gainful occupation chosen is for many a person an invitation to a wider acquaintance, or fellowship. Above and around the too-frequent will to gain the most and to give the least, many a hired man or the employer seize the opportunity to flock with others busied like them, and all these with still others in connected work, or with those met in buying and selling. And so it is among doctors and lawyers, among teachers and the clergy, with those in the same profession and with those they serve. The professional spirit also speaks of the public obligation to bear in mind the common welfare. Welcome will be the day when such a spirit masters all the professions and extends its rule into business and labour, into production and sale.

And other channels there are, too many to be described here—but too important to be left unnamed—the services for health, the hospital for the sick of mind or body, the libraries and museums, advanced schools, and universities. There are, too, the newspapers, the radio, and movies; the park and playground; the theatre, the hall of music, and the gallery of art. There is the post-office and telegraph. And there is law and the legislature, and the court of justice. These and others of their kind help the person to find his way to manhood and membership in his community. They offer him knowledge and appreciation of more than his biological promptings; he may be deterred from injuring others; and is defended against outrage; he is shown a thousand attractions—things both ugly and untrue; he is also shown things of beauty and honour. These press upon him and ask of him his affections, his fealty. His choice declares his distance along the way of reclamation.

These living social instruments are more than mere channels or conductors. They generate energy of their own and they transform the energy of others. What reaches a man through these various channels is of prime significance, and its quality depends largely on the character of the community from which so much of it issues. This character may, for short, be called the mind, the spirit of the community.

Each of these channels requires jealous care that the stream it carries may flow free and unpolluted. The family above all else must have inner strength and wisdom for its task. For rare indeed is the man whose mind, and especially the level of it we call spirit, does not bear the marks of his early home. And to-day, nearly the world over, it is weakening or falling apart. Hitler's marvels of ill were due not a little to taking the child as soon as possible from its home and shattering the home's influence.

III

But with all this attention to outward situations we must not overlook certain additional powers within the individual that are essential in his reclamation.

Highly significant among these powers within is imitation. By means of it he receives and transmits gains from thousands of years of others' experience. This has its risk and responsibility, as has the use of any power. Men actually pick and choose what they will imitate, whom they will imitate, but an indiscriminate refusal to imitate at all, as some have advised, were this possible, would mark one for a home of the feeble-minded.

Along with imitation, so important for reclaiming us, is sympathy with others, and some measure of fascination in their presence. Their effect on us is mildly hypnotic. We and they are in rapport; we are impelled, though not irresistibly, to heed what they say and do as they do. Shakespeare was open to a thousand other minds; as was Dante. So it was also with Lincoln. Originators must be imitators. But all that is offered them must be scrutinized, tested, worked over.

An important companion of sympathy and imitation is antipathy. The person defends himself against unwelcome oncomers. He challenges, he repels. Thus the person himself is never as clay on the potter's wheel. He not only resists pressure toward a certain form, but spontaneously bulges out to an opposite shape. It is as though the potter must, from moment to moment, hear the protest or consent of the substance he would shape. And out of this conjunction of imitation, sympathy and antipathy comes a real and working member of a community.

And the making of such members is no small achievement. For a community of such members, as has been seen, is the prerequisite for important creative work, including that of plain helpers and men of genius.

IV

Changes in men's understanding attachments and purposes are the core of reclamation. The schools need to discover and invent complements to facts and more facts. The transformation, the humanizing of the young, the making of men, must be ever in mind in training teachers and in appointing them. The press, the movies, the radio must be more inventive to overcome their sodden commerce and all else unbecoming a community that is both free and responsive to the common need. And so for every other device for speaking to the mind of man. With their special contributions to the value of life they are living instruments for continuing and bettering what is excellent in society, and of diminishing what is misshapen and pestilential.

Experimental science and economic production will be of help. But if we go the way of those who put their trust in these and in these alone, we shall fail. Blast furnaces and cyclotrons require us to master them by attachments to far greater objects, by purposes centred on these objects.

And these objects are not revealed by chemist's scales nor by psychological tests, but by a growing wisdom that accepts all that science offers and then presses on into a region not open to electronics or the most penetrating of telescopes.

This wisdom comes from the search for it by many in every age and land—the search for the good life. And those portions of the wisdom that a people holds to be of highest worth stand forth as obligations, as the voice of duty. The fulfilment of these obligations is given honour; and their violation disgrace. So supported, this wisdom becomes a power to hold men to whatever may be their degree of reclamation, and to spur them toward new attachments. A dignity, a majesty is thus given to obligation that is absent from mere maxims, known and approved. The way to the good life is darkened when men no longer clothe duty in something of the awe it had for Wordsworth and Kant alike, and think only of rights, prudence and enlightened self-interest. The good fight is then lost.

Now every high religion addresses itself to men's affections and aims, directing these to things held to be worthy of their love or abhorrence, worthy of their efforts to upbuild or destroy. And each high faith includes some portion of that whole that in this writing has been held essential. And in the faith of the Christ every man is urged to give his heart and his will to perfecting nothing less than the very whole—the man himself, his inner life especially; his fellow-man whoever and whatever he may be, whose well-being and advance are to be regarded as every whit as important as the man's own; and the community in which a divine purpose is more and more realized. This instruction, this briefing of adventurous wills has been among the chief instruments of recalamation in the West, and must be put to still more effective use in the future.

With this great means conjoined to all the rest here recounted, indeed heading them and many others that must occur to anyone—with these means and the will to use them, men cannot fail to penetrate far into the wide realm that is their goal.

SUCCESS AND FAILURE WITHIN NATIONS

'And what has come of all this power and effort to make real high aims and answer the dire need?' those will ask in scorn who see little but the avarice and dissension within their country. The failure rather than the success of reclamation stares out at many, and they see men struggling in vain with forces in and about them.

It must be acknowledged that the forces for the humane life have met stubborn resistance, and defeat after defeat—defeats acknowledged fully in previous chapters and not called strategic advances to the rear.

Realists, no less however, should recognize the fields won and held, to serve as bases for further gains. This on a grand scale has been part, the more significant part, of the plain truth when seen not to-day or yesterday in the shock of disaster, but in the light of centuries, of thousands of years. And all the while we shall be looking not only at our distance from the goal, but also at the distance from the ways of men at the beginning of our race's great adventure. An immensity of things unsuited to men has been cast out, and an immensity of what befits them secured. Even a partial account of it should put courage into the disheartened. The result is the more impressive, it will be remembered, because those who have gained but half their sight are leading the blind; the sick are ministering to the sick.

I

As was shown earlier, signal successes have been won not only in men's surroundings, but in men themselves, indeed in the very citadel of men's minds. With the indispensable help of gains in understanding, the work of transformation has reached into men's attachments or affections, and purposes. For the quality and scope of these are central in the work now under appraisal. And in this respect, men who are really civilized have come a long journey from their primitive estate. They have left clan or tribe and whatever preceded these, and each has become a member of a great company, a nation that, even if as small as Denmark or Norway, includes millions besides himself. They are his own people, and what they suffer and surmount affects him more deeply than do the like fortunes of any other nation. His emotions are stirred—of joy over his country's courage, and anger if the ill has come to it from some human source.

The man has thus become attached to a larger human object than ever was cared for by his most distant human ancestors. His appreciation of men has enlarged its compass. He has widened his loyalty. And his purposes, which always move with the attachments, now include the defence and advancement of these new companions along with himself. His loyalty has burst its primal narrow bounds.

With this enlarged human connection there has come to hosts of men an appreciation of larger aims, and an adoption of these aims as their own—to be just, and to have justice in the common

THE WILDS AND THEIR RECLAMATION 135

life; to have liberty and to assure to others as much of it as comports with the common welfare; not to live as anarchists and nihilists, but to be governed by the freely expressed will of the majority of the citizens; and to have personal and public integrity and fair play prevail. Men care for these ideas, and are less and less content to see them trodden down.

Men have come to appreciate, to hold fast, and maintain many a form of service unknown to early man—services rendered by those specially prepared—not only to the long-recognized professions of lawyer, physician, teacher and religious leader, but also of the trained nurse, and of the experts in nutrition and public health; of landscape gardener, and tree surgeons; of farm advisers and psychiatrists, and on through an almost endless list.

And with our appreciation of such services, most of us have lost what attachment we may have had for gaining our ends by violence, lying, cheating and all intended inhumanity, including crime. These have become repugnant; we have come to disown them as enemies of what we hold dear.

Under our very eyes we see such a change in the attachment to war. The plain man, under the impact of one or both World Wars, no longer feels as did Ruskin—not to name with him many Prussian minds—that war is the source of many if not all great goods. Instead it is abhorred as the cruelest and least reasonable of all men's deeds, and they are setting their wills to root it out.

Such are some instances of what has been done to the very centre of men's minds, giving them new things to prize, to support with anger and affection; to maintain with might and main. This is a cumulative result of age-long experience and of struggle for the good life.

II

Great advances have been made also in the realm of our natural impulses or drives. Their intolerable disorder and disproportion had already been lessened in many a savage community; and among civilized men the work has been carried much farther. In multitudes of plain men and women, indeed in most of them there is established a large measure of hearty inward self-government. The increased popular attention in our day to emotional complexes and repressions, frustration and projection, and to insanity and crime—all excellent and fruitful as much of this new attention is—has concealed from many of us the even temper, the sound minds, the hearty impulses of millions.

Let us glance at an instance or two of the ground won. The readiness to take and appropriate whatever may please one even though in another's possession—this acquisitive impulse so often the occasion of anger and jealousy, of fighting and robbery, has for most men been tempered and counter-balanced into a beneficent activity within every community.

Not a few may smile at this. For there is in the purpose and action of some trade unions, some manufacturers, and some merchants so large a remnant of cave-ways that many of us fail to see the advance we have made and suffer the illusion that our own economic life, whether it be of New York or Moscow, is but pre-savage acquisitiveness on the grand scale.

The fact is, however, that instead of taking whatever they can, as would pre-savages lacking the first trace of reclamation, the most of us to-day, billions strong, far and near, get what we cannot produce by giving goods, services or money in recompense. And violators of this rule are pounced upon and often prevented or punished.

This is an immense gain, without which the weak would be entirely at the mercy of the strong; the strong would despise and virtually enslave their dependents; production, distribution and the spirit of the community as we know them would not exist. Nor for most of us is official power or the honour of guardians and trustees ever secretly for sale. Not the law and prison, but self-judgment and repugnance hold us back.

III

Further of sex, enough has been said earlier of sex to indicate that even this masterful activity has with most persons been brought nearer to what is humane. Even when Walter Savage Landor at a dance exclaimed, in effect, of a woman across the room whom he had never seen before: 'There is the prettiest woman in the room. By Gad, I'll marry her!' and soon did so, repenting at leisure; yet he was not seizing her then and there and having his will, by a 'drive' untouched by education and the social code. With all the license of the day, probably but a smallest portion of any community has remained wholly impervious to what is civil here.

And finally of these native impulses, even pugnacity and violence, which in our world to-day seem to many the very denial of all success, raging as unrestrained as any prairie fire—pugnacity and violence do in fact illustrate our control of wild natural impulse. Pugnacity in perhaps nine out of ten civilized men and women is still alive and is expressed, but in all private, personal, face-to-face relations—which by far are the most trying of all—there are now relatively few attempts at bodily injury. And in perhaps eight of every ten, there is no attempt at any serious injury of any kind, save to the feelings or to pride. The extension of the community from the family to the nation has softened the mutual behaviour and the will of men in tens of millions, leaving the primal passions to be fostered and implemented for mass slaughter, when pugnacity is aroused between nations.

Between members of the same community, this is clearly true, both for individuals and for bodies of men. In all governed communities our natural endowment of friendly, sympathetic, social impulses have been fostered and implemented, until in multitudes, indeed with the most of civilized men in every generation there is a government in the individual himself, as well as around him, that holds him and his fellows together in respect and co-operation. What seemed the weaker powers in man's endowment have artfully won lasting victories over his combative, his divisive powers. Every community in health testifies to this achievement.

IV

Collaboration and the abounding benefits that issue from it are ours to-day. We and men before us have built up a vast fellow-working for benefits that are shared. Savages never achieved this, much less those with an endowment even less reclaimed.

This immense concert of work is not only a great acquisition in itself—not inborn in us, as in bees and ants—but is the most powerful of instruments for still further gains.

For in the most advanced nations each citizen, naturally irascible and contentious, has been brought to act with millions of others to maintain political government to protect this co-operation—a co-operation which gains for him much of what he desires by so working as to meet some of the desires of others. And in turn these others labour for him.

And added to this multitude of benefits passed visibly from person to person, mainly by exchange, are the abounding goods held in common, produced in common. These goods include a mutual consideration and goodwill between men, and a reach of minds toward what exceeds the past and present; goods that include and create the ideas and purposes, the behaviour and social instruments of a well-ordered society, intent on justice and mercy; creative of knowledge, of liberty, and of obligation; of wonder and reverence.

All these aims have in part been fulfilled; far indeed from what is seen in the child, or the savage. And with most individuals there has come an inner government.

v

We have seen the changes in human attachments and purposes as earlier described—the artful encouragement and restraint, for instance, of our native impulsions; also the expanded collaboration and the manifold harvest it has brought us, of food and comfort, of rights, privileges and opportunities. All these have made for better inner powers both to command and to obey. Further, man's natural endowment, as we have seen, does not include an inner government over our host of unruly powers. Many a long mile, however, have we advanced toward what is needed for men who are to become governed, yet free and creative. This control is another kind of gain that has been added.

And among these advances is the limitation of the despotic rule of some particular power within the person that brooks no inner rivals. This despotic power, it is true, is, at times, little better than anarchy that foils productive effort by the individual. So we should acknowledge, though with scant praise, the countless persons who have subjected all that is in them to the single desire for money or personal power or social position, or for science, or art, to the virtual death of all else. To the extent that the human mind is under such tyranny we may hold the gains from it as bought at too high a price.

Many in our day and in days past had within them a wiser sway. This is true of a multitude of renowned scientists, poets, philosophers, and leaders in religion, and is no less true of a vast company of the less gifted. Instances of their kind are known to everyone—a joy to their friends, kind to strangers, unbelievably capable of small services, and with eye never far from what is heroic and sublime. In a person so governed, each of his powers has its part, its office, and all work together as a reliable, sagacious and generous whole. The well-governed mind stands before us concretely in Emerson, whose serene union of rarest gifts—of understanding, and sensitivity, of attachment and purpose—found expression in his writings and in his life-long fidelity to himself and all men and to their great federation with one another and with the Over Soul.

VIII

RECLAIMING THE INTERNATIONAL MIND

THE MIND THAT STILL PREVAILS

THE attitude of nations toward one another creates the most pressing of all the problems of our time. This momentous area of men's minds remains the least affected by the forces of reclamation. Here our natural impulses show forth nearly all their original unfitness for civilized communal life. And there exists, as seen earlier, a condition that brings war after war. The cure, the only cure and prevention, is a more inclusive community of nations. The community is now our direst need, and calls for all that is in mankind for generative ability. The task is of immense but not disheartening difficulty. The labour required of us is of a kind in which men have been engaged since the beginning—that of enlarging the area of conduct in which men treat one another as members of one community. The growing aims and the growing means to fulfil these aims, recently described, need not be here repeated; for they are substantially the same in reclaiming the international region as in winning each lesser region from its wildness. And yet there are important differences, and not a little may properly be said to meet the special needs of this portentous arid terrain.

I

In any international organization—as, indeed, in any other body of men—the character of the mental forces in control of it is more important than its particular form of organization. Members of an ill-planned body who nevertheless are stoutly resolved to do the work in hand, are likely to go far; while those in an organization with an excellent design, but who themselves are lukewarm or antagonistic, will hardly move an inch. The British Commonwealth of Nations, for example, has but a shadowy structure. The Statute of Westminster is largely an agreement as to what it is *not*. But the Member Nations of this Commonwealth have a mind in common for a fairly definite and difficult task, and they continue at this task decade after decade with signal success.

The League of Nations, on the contrary, had a carefully wrought form of organization, and yet was unequal to its task, because the League's mental structure was unequal to that task. The League did lesser things admirably; its members were of a mind for these. No defect of the Covenant prevented action where there was a will for action. But against Japan in 1931 and 1932 there was a will only to inquire and to discuss what was reported, but no concerted will then to stop Japan; nor to stop Italy in 1935; nor Germany in 1938. If the Covenant had been perfect, and the members had still their sicklied resolution, the result would have been the same. And likewise of numberless other bodies of men.

In general, then, organization is indispensable in any important undertaking, and the organization must have some form. But far less thought, less effort, should go into niceties of form in the organization than into the forces of mind that shall prevail in the whole. No virtues of plan and elevation can outweigh sheer perversity of thought and volition; and also no virtues of concerted purpose and understanding will come to naught because of an ill-drafted article or two on parchment. Neither of the two aspects of the whole should, however, suffer neglect; each needs the other. A shapely mind is at its best in a shapely brain and frame. But an international organization almost hollow, in the region where a right mind should be, is nearer the abyss than is a company of nations which collectively lacks a hand or a foot but whose mind is fit for the work.

In the foundation of such a structure there must be steel-strong psychic reinforcement. And to disclose the main features of this reinforcement in the foundation and in the superstructure will be the purpose of this and the following chapters. There will be an attempt to decide in the light of observed fact and the nations' need, the forces of mind necessary for the work in hand, necessary also to withstand the forces of mind which will oppose such an enterprise. Such a study, it is to be hoped, will contribute to the fortune of the greatest undertaking of statecraft of our or any earlier epoch.

II

Among the highly important facts that throughout should stand clear before us are the mental characteristics of the society of nations as it now is and long has been. A view of these—however blurred the view be in detail, as from an aeroplane—is essential to our study; for only in this way can we know the nature of our organization. In a sense, the organization is at once both physician and patient. To do its work well, it must be the instrument by which its members heal themselves. What, then, is true of the society as a whole, in spite of the endless contrasts among the nations that compose it?

Sorry indeed at first sight does the society of nations appear. Powerful adverse forces are in control. But happier forces, we shall all the while remember, are waiting to be strengthened into dominance. Otherwise our case would be hopeless.

The nations are all marked alike in this; *each of them immoderately appreciates itself and immoderately depreciates all or most of the others*. A nation may feel friendly toward some, it may rightly appraise the might or the intelligence of some, and of some it may be the foe. But a nation never in its corporate ways of mind habitually sees the full worth of other nations.

Of the United States, for example, the people as a whole are confident of their nation's superiority to all others, in its power, way of life, its public institutions; in freedom from the animosities found elsewhere, in the will to be the good neighbour. Its shortcomings are at times recognized, but knowledge is kept in some dark cupboard of the mind. This almost spotless self-appraisal of the United States is found not only among the ignorant.

A friend of mine, college-bred and widely travelled, held the United States to be the most peace-loving of all nations; and an admiral of ours once said to a small group of us seriously that the

United States was on a plane far above that of other countries and should not enter any organization for the general security, but should stand apart until other nations attained our level.

Nor is this a trait of Americans only. Some years ago a young Chinese gentleman in a small class of mine was asked whether the Chinese of to-day regarded themselves as the greatest of peoples. For a moment he hesitated as puzzled to find a reason for the question, so self-evident was its answer. 'Why, of course,' he said simply, and no more. Faced with a like question about his own people, many a Briton, or Frenchman, or Russian would doubtless have known, if not shown, a somewhat similar incomprehension. The Germans and the Japanese carried out this attitude in a way hitherto never conceived, clothing it with legend and mystery. 'Only a German can understand this matter,' said a high-placed Nazi official in Berlin, at a certain point in our conversation, he doubtless noticing in me some lack of zeal for what he said.

III

The counterpart of such inordinate self-appreciation is, that each nation habitually depreciates other nations, although this attitude does not, as we have seen, exclude some appreciation of some others.

War and defeat in war may inflame the mistrust and antipathy, but do not originate them. Such feelings have long possessed the Argentine toward the 'collossus of the north' which has never waged war upon her. But the United States, while desiring the trade of Argentina, has never had at heart much care for her economic welfare, and has wounded her pride. Malicious damage is not necessary to make enemies. To look the other way, as one passes, is enough. But openly to wear what another thinks is his jewel is more effective for animosity. Animosity here is more than feeling, for into it go thoughts, emotions, impulses and steady aims. Its features stare out from nearly every act of any member of the society of the nations, be that member Bulgaria or Greece, or Chile; be it Russia, or the United States. It passes over into a fixed policy favourable to the nation itself, and almost reckless or malign toward others. From what at first may seem but a harmless egotism arise delusion and deadly injustice, although these are tempered in no small degree within the internally Warless Circle. Thus our actual society of nations remains far from a true community. An adverse cast of mind deepens the moat about each member, and holds high the drawbridge over it.

MISSHAPEN OFFSPRING OF THAT MIND

I

The self-regard and alienation just described are expressed partly in changing and impulsive ways, suited to the hour. But they also utter themselves in certain kinds of action which remain constant through the centuries, in storm and fair weather. So persistent, so clear in outline, and of such cardinal importance are these forms of conduct, that they may well be called institutions of the international society.

The first of these established modes of expressing self-love and detachment from others is the sovereignty and independence of each nation, an institution cherished, and jealously guarded by every nation, at all times and everywhere. It was never absent from the deliberations from which issued the League of Nations. Small nations were as anxious about it as the great. In whatever they do (it is made clear) the nations act as sovereign; nothing said or done shall in any way impair their Sovereignty. They approach one another, crowned, in ermine, heralded by trumpets, as on a Field of the Cloth of Gold. Thus the nations are not free to conduct their mutual affairs with common sense and homely wisdom, as burghers may for the order and trade of the town. Each nation must fix its thought above all else on its regal dignity, its monarchic rights. Any proposal for the defence, or health of all nations must first be pared down to fit this treasured thing.

We here confront no physical obstacle which dynamite can blast away, but something more stubborn, existing in the minds of men, in the thinking, the loyalty, the will of plain men and diplomats alike.

II

The second of these established ways of mind in nations is their effort for the highest possible degree of *economic* independence —of economic autarky—most evident in nations of great power.

In these nations it seldom is allowed free course. It restricts, but does not completely prevent imports from abroad, and only indirectly does it restrict exports. The motive here is mixed, but in it is the desire that the nation be the master of its fate, in both war and peace. But whatever degree of independence is thus gained is gained at a price. The clear advantages of exchange are lessened, the wealth available in the world's markets is reduced, and life is on a lower economic level. Serious loss, serious injustice thus may befall the great nations as well as the small.

Nearly all this is an instituted way of thought and action which cannot lightly be cast aside by any nation for itself alone. It exists as a network in which almost all are enmeshed. It restricts the freedom alike of those nations that disapprove it; and of those who give it their heart and hand.

III

Further, among these established ways of mutual behaviour is anarchy; the society of the nations is an ungoverned society. There has long been international law, it is true, and early in the 1920's there was created an international court of justice. These, however, are but fragments of government, not government itself. There is no standing communal power to arrest a nation charged with a grave international offence; no power to hail the nation into court, try it, and punish it if guilty. Nor is there the organized power to perform the other functions of government. Each nation by itself is a governed community; but not so is the society of which each is a member. And since they maintain this state of things, each is a true anarchist in a great region of its conduct; every nation—the United States, Great Britain, Russia and all others who plume themselves on their international virtues. Thus the international society denies itself all those benefits that are possible only under government—a fuller measure of justice, a fuller production and exchange of goods, an adequate and permanent defence against the private use of force; and a freer co-operation to provide much more than all of these together. Nations make treaties, they sign conventions, and some of them are fairly well-behaved toward other nations. And yet each, deep in its psychic constitution, is averse to being ruled even though it have a voice in the rule.

This anarchy established, or instituted, from the dawn of history, is a towering obstacle to more than the rudiments of the world community and its needed organization.

IV

Still further, there is the institution of war, the fitting companion of the institutions already named. War and all the other institutions express in their several ways the mutual psychic detachment of nations, their mutual alienation.

There have been quarter-hearted attempts to end war indirectly by limiting the national armament. War itself has officially and formally been condemned and renounced. But as long as the nations cling passionately to these other institutions which are the boon companions of war, war will be their bitter portion. And so long as this continues, and their lives are spent in preparing for war, in waging war, and in recovery from war only to have the cycle upon them anew, there will be powerful incentives to strong national armaments and allies; along with heightened threats and fears and rivalries for power, readily running to war after war.

The nations inevitably cling to war so long as they cling to sovereignty, economic non-co-operation and anarchy. The organization will feel the divisive effect of this national warfare. So long as national wars continue, the nations must all the while be on guard against the desertion or outright treachery of some of their fellow-nations in any global organization. Thus co-operation is enfeebled; its aim befogged.

Along with all these, indeed interwoven with them, is the low level of morals in the international society. This level is established, is instituted. It is not unopposed, however. The rudiments

V

of mutual obligation are, here and there, felt and are fulfilled. There are the beginnings of conscience. In times of disaster to some foreign people—from flood, fire, or earthquake; from plague or famine—sympathy and care go out generously to the stricken.

And yet in the society generally, frequent are the violations of what is solemnly and freely promised. Not a few of the nations of high standing are ready, on occasion, to lie, to cheat, to steal, and to kill. So much is there of all this, that the nations breathe a poisonous vapour which paralyses their co-operation at a thousand points. Conscience and obligation are no invention of Puritans; they are fundamentals of fruitful co-operation, without which no real community can exist and satisfy its central needs.

Such are a few of the established ways of mind and conduct, which properly may be called institutions of the existing international society. They give effect to the immense self-regard of nations, and their immense mutual disregard. Sovereignty, political independence, and a high degree of economic independence, together with anarchy, war, and morals at their lowest—these great institutions stand sullen to defeat our desired result. These are indeed dour surroundings for the needed creative work.

FORMS EMERGING FROM THE MIST

I

The forces of mind which prevail in the existing society of nations have been reviewed. But these are not the sole forces there; others—as indicated repeatedly in this writing—are present everywhere, even though they are not the ruling powers. And what is called for is a revolution of the public mind. For this we must openly conspire, with no less tireless ingenuity than is now devoted to the equipment and strategy of disrupting our common life. It will come, and it will change the face of history.

Only later will the full drama of it unfold. It will be no revolution bearing the name of some day, or month, or year, for it will be slow to run its course. Indeed, this revolution has been actual now for decades.

II

For in reviewing a wide range of evidence in earlier chapters it appeared that the violence between nations, as well as between other bodies of men and between individuals, follows a simple law that may roughly be stated thus. *Violence between men varies in frequency inversely with the strength of the psychic ties of community between them.* Where men are mentally held together by the many subtle yet strong bonds of fellow membership in a community they may differ seriously in interest and purpose; they may dispute and be angry and may hate; they may carry their difference into court, and thereafter hate each other for life. But rarely do such men resort to violence to life and property. Something within both of them conspires with forces surrounding them to restrain them from these extremes. Such is the effect of a dynamic social process at work from infancy to old age, acting together with forces resident in men by nature. And the community, the fellowship, which has this profound effect is not only a town or village. It begins as a family and widens through friends and associates to one's countryside and city out into one's state, one's nation. In some individuals, because of hard facts within and without them, their ties of mind with others are few and short, confined to some child or pal or woman.

So it is, also, between most of our nations, though in varying degrees and directions. The member-nations of the Warless Circle, for example, of a previous chapter, have greatly reduced the devisive forces between one another, while leaving these forces still powerful to hold many of these members far apart from many outside the Circle. Across this line intercourse, contact, friction, have far outrun communal ties.

Those, however, who refuse to be dismayed by the magnitude of the work required, who disregard their repugnance to this

RECLAIMING THE INTERNATIONAL MIND 149

or that nation, such persons will help to strengthen the ties of mutual interest, mutual need, mutual benefit, which are the beginnings of the community—and are the enemies of international anarchy and confusion.

The task of the organization we sorely need, then, is clear. It must remove as rapidly as possible whatever obstacles it can now and later remove—obstacles to a common life of the nations. And it must labour with might and main for all that is a part of the foundation and superstructure of a community. From this, in the degree it is attained, will come to the nations not only liberation from violence, but freedom they never have known, to labour with creative skill for many a good they had never hoped to have.

The quality and magnitude of the work ahead thus begins to appear dimly before us.

III

Is not this a millennial idea, of no practical bearing to-day and to-morrow? Not at all. The creative power in men when many are united in a great purpose, so often illustrated in this writing, still exists, and is shaping special instruments for the international task. And there exists that company of nations, called the Warless Circle, that stands as a nucleus for the needed development. In this powerful group is a strengthening determination to organize the forces for peace in the world. The League of Nations, weak as was its communal mind, was from its beginning able to stop or prevent small but highly dangerous wars. It established the World Court of Justice. It set financially crippled countries on their feet. War prisoners and refugees were restored to their homelands. For a while the brain and muscles of scores of nations were actually controlled by the thought (almost smothered in thoughts against it) of a Community working for the common good; and they did redoubtable deeds.

And now the United Nations represents the will of many nations to put an end to national warfare, and to maintain instruments for pacific effort—the Court of International Justice, the

Labour Organization, the Economic and Social Council, and much more.

Thus the beginnings of the corporate mind needed for our organization to be activated by that mind are no longer mere forms in cloudland. They are generators of energy in a troubled time. They can and must undergird the agreements signed and the institutions established to fulfill these agreements.

THE MIND THAT MUST BE ACHIEVED

I

The beginnings of the required mind as just seen, is already a reality, a generator of energy among nations. We should now see what it must become, in order to fulfill its high office.

There must be as a part of that mind the purpose to defend each member by all the members in concert. This is the first requirement. The organization, the community as it comes into being, must regard an attack on any member nation, great or small, near or far, as an attack on all, as a thrust at the very life of the community itself. And it must be prepared to come instantly to the defence of that member. This purpose must be shrewd and steadfast. The might of the community—its economic, political, military, and moral might—must be, not potential merely, but actual, girded and visibly superior to that of any nation or nations likely to rise against it. It must possess this ready power, not only in order to defeat conspirators, but also to give confidence to its loyal members. They must, without shadow of doubt, know themselves more secure behind the sword and shield of their community than they could ever be by any separate powers of their own.

This will involve provision for military instruments—on land and sea, and in the air—a will for this, and a will also for standing provision to throw against aggression at an early stage the community's full civil might, economic, political, and moral, along with the formal judgment of a court of law and of an informed public mind.

The effectual will for defence of each by all, there must be. For without it, our organized body of nations will soon find itself rent by attempts at separate defence, by special economic, political, and martial arrangements with some members to the neglect of others. Such was the early misfortune of the League of Nations. 'Power politics' by the Great, and the scramble of the small for great allies, is the alternative to a united defence. Benighted are those who would have neither communal defence *nor* 'power politics' in the organization; they must choose the one or the other. And power politics, the inevitable result of inadequate defence in common, will in a hundred ways obstruct beneficent co-operation.

II

Besides the purpose to defend, *there will be a continuing purpose for economic and other forms of the common welfare.* The community will be intelligently bent to foster trade, and to lower and finally to demolish the intentional obstructions to trade. The Scandinavian nations have borne this in mind. For although they have similar goods to be marketed abroad—which easily might bring fierce economic competition—yet they have, instead, put their heads together to co-operate for a place in the world's markets. In like temper, the United States ended the restrictions on mutual trade which the States had imposed before they were united. And they became thereby the richer. This is but one of a community's ways to wealth. The purpose gradually to achieve this and other economic benefits to all members, will mean also a purpose to maintain international instruments to effect this purpose.

And beyond economic benefits in common, there will be a continuing purpose for a still broader welfare that includes health, relief from flood, fire, earthquake, pestilence and famine; includes also suitable conditions in factory and mine, on farm and shipboard, and has a will for international decency and morals.

III

Essential to the mind of our organization is, also, a growing will for justice between member and member. Such a will is all interwoven with purposes already mentioned—namely to defend each member and to have regard for his welfare. For it will be an injustice to its members if our body of nations fails to protect them and to add what it can to their prosperity. So much, then, is a beginning of what they would have a right to expect.

It is the right of every nation, moreover, that its treaties be inviolate. Every signatory of a treaty is injured, suffers an injustice, when a solemn agreement between him and another is treated as a scrap of paper. The organization cannot afford to be indifferent to this kind of injury.

Further, it is the right of every nation that international law be inviolate. The society as a whole has too long been careless of violations of this right. The mind of a community of the nations will be to prevent these infractions, these injustices. For they rend the fabric which should shelter all.

But justice does not come by strong will alone, nor by will and hands. The proper tools must be in hand. Law, court, and police and the indispensable means of justice. A body of law we already have, and a court of law, which should be ready, and at work. These must be bettered for the use of our new body of nations. But there still is wanting, any adequate power of legislation, any adequate power to summon before the bar, and to give effect to the court's decision. The purpose to have these must exist as soon as may be. Such is but a smallest reflection of the needed will for justice in our community.

IV

Further, *there must be a persisting undaunted purpose to make of the society of the nations a governed community*. At present, as we saw, the idea of being governed is repugnant to almost all nations. The society, blind lover, see little but beauty in its old mate, this hag, anarchy. Dire suffering beyond anything that has yet come of this horrible mating may still be needed for a change of heart.

The purposes already seen to be indispensable forces of mind in our organization bring us, it is true, toward government. But they are purposes to have only *some* of the functions to government, not government itself. They are great indispensables, but not enough.

In our international body the organs of defence must be at one with the organs of law; and both of these must receive support from the organs of economic health and give support in return. And in the end there must be the purpose to bring these and other organs and functions into mutual support, and into concerted fulfilment of the central aims of the organization. In whatever measure the nations become intolerant of the international anarchy, they must tolerate and desire this communal control.

V

Still more is required. *There must be the desire and will for mutual understanding among the member nations.* This includes acquaintance, a knowledge of their best qualities and not only of their worst. But acquaintance is not enough; for neighbours may know much, and yet hate each other. An increasing degree of mutual appreciation, and active good will are essential; for these are among the psychic ties of community; they make peoples feel that they belong together, bear a common name, and gladly include each other in saying 'we' and 'our'.

The purpose to have mutual understanding involves a will to do what creates understanding. Ways and means must be found, instruments skilfully fashioned. And here the past helps us. For there were established in the years between two World Wars international instututions for this very purpose—the League's Organization for Intellectual Co-operation. And the United Nations, too, has provided for such work.

A will for mutual acquaintance, appreciation, and active good will, must be a part of the corporate mind of our commonwealth.

VI

The corporate mind, moreover, must have in it a loyalty of the members to their international community; a sense of its worth, a concern for its welfare. It has already been said here that the community as a working whole must be solicitous for the well-being of each of its members. A reciprocal solicitude, of each member for the community as a working whole, is no less required. The nation member will find it not wholly impossible to feel some measure of zeal for the well-being of the great organized company to which the nation has pledged its faith. All manner of fears will arise, however, but our own history should quiet some of them. Virginia, for instance did not lose its individuality in becoming one of the States of our Union; nor did Scotland, in becoming a part of the United Kingdom. The old loyalty remained, but in time found its place within the larger loyalty.

The ties that lead to loyalty may at first be not loyalty itself. They may begin—perhaps as ties of sheer prudence on each member's part, as nothing but ties of cold calculation of profit and loss to the nation itself. But death knocks at the door of any commonwealth whose members continue in nothing beyond the book-keeping of self-love. Self-love should remain. But with it there must be a clear sense of the intrinsic worth and dignity of the enfolding community, and a will to maintain it, and for its sake, to suffer loss.

VII

Beyond what some would understand by loyalty, but quite within its meaning for others, the needed forces of mind in the organization will include the members' *obligations to this greater community, obligations which will be an enlargement of conscience*. Certain acts, it will urgently be felt, *must be done*; and certain other acts, it will be felt with like urgency *must never be done, so disgraceful are they*. And this sense of urgency may at first spring only from external legislation and the fear of sanctions; but in time it will arise from the members' mind's own inner command. But as with the obligation of the citizen to his country, so here: the obligations may be disregarded by one or another member nation, but not without inner distress. The United States will long be disquieted in national conscience by her sale of oil and iron to Japan by which Japan slaughtered Chinese and laid waste their lands.

There is corporate obligation, a corporate conscience, which begins weak and ineffectual, but may become strong. And a strengthened conscience our organization will need to hold it to its work, and give it endurance and majesty. But, it should be repeated, this conscience must be reciprocal—a force in the community, an organized body, and governing its behaviour toward each of its members—a force also in each of these members, governing its thought, sentiment, and behaviour toward the encompassing community.

VIII

In the organization, further, *there must prevail in each member nation the will to co-operate with all other members for the common good.* Each must contribute, from its own mind, this psychic force to the corporate mind; and the corporate mind in its turn must foster this force in the minds of nations. This purpose to co-operate must be conjoined with each of the other purposes here recounted. For unless the purpose to defend and to have the instruments of defence, be conjoined *with the purpose to co-operate* for this defence, the purpose to defend will inevitably fail: there will never be adequate defence.

And likewise, of the purpose to have justice, the purpose to increase the nations' wealth, and all the other purposes necessary to corporate mind. By co-operation the nations have come into great international possessions—their system of communications, of telephone, and radio; transportation, by land, sea and air; and of commerce by which across national boundaries, come food, and materials, come machinery and all manner of other goods. By co-operation the nations have fought pestilence, the slave trade, piracy, and the traffic in vice; and by co-operation they protect one another's rights of property in the products of factory, of intellect, and of art, on foreign soil. By co-operation the nations have brought international law into being, along with the beginnings of adjudication, law-enforcement, and administration. Co-operation does not exclude work by nations single-handed. But there is much work which profoundly affects all nations in common, which no nation can do for itself, and for which all must work in concert. The unreluctant acceptance of this truth, and the will to give it effect, must become an international axiom, taken as a matter of course, relied upon as, in our domestic life, we rely on others and they on us. Every community is a magic web of co-operation. In the international organization, likewise, the will to co-operate must become second nature as this body becomes our Community, our Commonwealth.

HOW TO ACHIEVE THIS MIND

I

Roughly there have been sketched some main features of the mind that must control our body of nations. And many a reader may well ere now have been saying: ' Well and good; but how are we ever to have this fair mind in control? Whence shall it come, and who will give it place and power? ' This is a fair question and something toward an answer should be attempted. It hardly need be said that the mind here required will never come of itself! never by mere wishing, and waiting. Only hard labour—labour hard, enduring, and concerted—can bring our result.

Now, while the task is far beyond any labour of Hercules, and it would be a disservice to understate it, yet also it should not be exaggerated. No miracle is asked of us. We are required, great as the requirement is, only to extend farther a work begun long ago and now far advanced. The nation, each nation by its very existence, is in fact beyond the mid-stage of an almost incredible construction which began with the family, and then extended into clan and tribe, into countryside and village, until it passed from city to nation and beyond. Step by step, men have been transformed in mind and nerve and muscle from creatures that could trust and co-operate with only a handful of men into creatures who could hold themselves from violence and co-operate within a larger and larger circle; until in a nation of to-day, most of its citizens have accepted millions on millions of men —strangers most of them—as men that need not be feared or hated.

II

It is a long journey farther, but no impossible journey, to a community of such nations as now can think and work together on a few vital matters, and then on, to include more and more. Suddenly extended communication and transport, and a sudden increase in common need for protection against man's inventive genius for destruction, now make possible a velocity of advance that was impossible a half century ago.

The task is, in fact more than half done. And to do the unfinished half we have better tools, more power, a deeper sense of need, and a stouter will than ever before.

But our task requires more than the knowledge given in most of our schools and colleges, although all this knowledge and still more of it, must be ours. The work will not be well done without renovated ideas and conclusions, with thinking flint-tipped, sent arrow-straight. But erudition gives no assurance of hitting the mark. I know and value a distinguished scientist who is as blind as any suckling to the value of what must be done. His emotions, his sentiments, his dogged hold on ancient creed about human nature hold him in their grip. He needs new knowledge, but he is now proof against the special knowledge he needs.

Encrusted habits of thinking, of antipathy and attachment, of fear and confidence, of effort and inertia, need patient and skilled re-conditioning. To illustrate, the fear lest our nation, by the new enterprise, lose some of its liberty of action must be tempered by an intenser fear of still greater losses if we do not beforehand pledge to our community of nations sufficient of our wealth and manhood and all manner of skill against a new World War and a long line of wars thereafter. Patriotism, also, that too often bars the way, must be made tolerant—even desirous—of a larger loyalty. Furthermore, the dislike, the distrust, of this and that foreign country must not be allowed to prevent us from uniting our will with theirs for our common good.

III

But to re-shape and toughen our minds for membership in our Great Commonwealth, the work should be, not hit or miss, but systematic. And for this, we may well recall our view of the society of the nations as it actually is, and particularly of its cast of mind. The work to be done must begin there; it deals with the society as it is, with its actual thought and passion, and purpose. Much must be kept there, much now there must be torn down and new things built in their place. Much stands square across the way to a great body of nations dominated by the mind of a community.

For we remember the puffed-up self-regard of these nations, and their gaunt, sickly regard for others. Self-will and ill-will curse the whole neighbourhood. For out of this overweaning self-regard and alienation, issue an array of institutions that, like mountain ranges, make Balkan-like the psychic terrain the world over. There is national sovereignty and political independence. together with all practicable economic independence. Further, there is anarchy, and a level of morals between many nations, that would befit a crew of pirates.

Education and a hundred devices beyond what this commonly means must undermine these barriers as well as the excess of self-regard and the excess of alienation from others. Construction here must follow, or rather must accompany, the sapping and mining—using old ways, and discovering new, to counterbalance self-regard with regard for fellow-nations, and to bridge the psychic chasm. And with this would be an ardour for the fundamentals of common life—for the unbroken promises, the decencies, the loyalties, of a commonwealth. This work of down-tearing and upbuilding must be done. It means life for the organized community.

IV

As to the means and manner of this great work, they are endless in number and diversity. No person should refuse enlistment in it, though many indeed will not move a finger for it. The way to learn is to teach. Families, as many families as will volunteer, should become instruments. And schools, of every grade and kind, should add what they can. Others should feel themselves elected to do and give, to use all manner of opportunities and devices. The owners, editors, and writers of newspapers and magazines, the authors and publishers of books —these hold an office here that is second only to that of parents. And high also is the responsibility of those who lead in the organizations of labour, and manufacturers, miners and farmers, of the owners and managers of capital; all these must learn and teach, to dovetail their interests, their habits, into a larger world. Leaders in religion must see to it that men's hunger of spirit, while transcending the realm of mind here studied, should not be wholly apart from it. No decent endeavour, public or private, can well go placidly about its business, detached from this undertaking that touches the brain and heart of all humanity. Each nation and all within it should, as in wartime, but now for a larger purpose, be called to the colours.

But the organized community of nations should have its own special means to prosper this work. It must help constantly to make known the facts that bear importantly on the new enterprise; to make known its purpose and progress in order that it be understood, be intelligently supported by its members. The United nations and its organ, the Economic and Social Council, must carry on and even better the work of Intellectual Co-operation done within the League and outside of it. The successes of the *International Labour Organization* may instruct us here. It became a power, not only in economics and politics, but in much else. By unconcealed indirection, it shaped thought and purpose in governments and peoples to do right things for men, women, and children, near and far.

v

Thus we come again to mutual understanding among member nations as a power not far from greatest in our community's mind. We may well go to Scandinavia for instruction. The nations there gave, in earlier days, as little promise of what they now are to one another, as the worst nations among us. Through centuries they warred on each other; they conquered and oppressed; they were treacherous; Danes killed Swedish hostages. And yet in time they mastered the art of mutual understanding. This did not come because they are of the same race and are neighbours. Elsewhere there are implacable national foes who are of the same race and are near neighbours. But the Scandinavians learned to deal with their situation. They had the audacity to learn from their oppressors; even while hating each other, they worked with each other. Reluctantly, doubtless, they held back their hands from deadly injury; they tempered their animosity. Acts of justice speak a language understood in any land. This language they used with one another. Later, with clear intent, they sought to know each other's way of life, literature and songs, history, laws, and ideals. They also learned much from actual co-operation to make less hurtful, more helpful, to each other their legislation, their economics, and their foreign policy. And in a hundred other ways they built bulwarks against their old violent self-will, and built bridges across their distrust, their alienation.

For our enterprise greater than theirs the obstacles are of the same kind, to be overcome by a like ingenuity and persistence.

For we men are not only adaptive to our environment, as are the beasts for the most part. We can, if we will—and actually do in thousands of ways—lay rough hands on our environment, both material and social, we dig into it, upturn it, and make of it something better adapted to the full play of our thwarted powers. Our international enterprise is precisely of this revolutionary character. The nations, essentially humane in their domestic life, have for thousands of years felt compelled to adapt themselves externally to social surroundings that are profoundly inhumane, since these surroundings are anarchic, given over to violent self-will. Many nations have at last grown intolerant of this chaos and are gaining in clear resolve to transform it into something befitting their great endowment. They at last are aware that their environment, their relations with one another, are inhospitable beyond endurance, and need not remain so, but can be made hospitable and bounteous in opportunity for creative work.

It is within our power, and it must be our will, to extend into this outlying wasteland of the human spirit, the creative action, including the reclamation, that has been the theme of all this writing. Thus we will enjoy the fruit of a watered and fertile soil.

THE GREATEST OF ALL ARTS

In strangely varied ways man announces himself to be—in Sir Thomas Browne's words—'that great and true *Amphibium*', for he lives in the world of the animals, and also in a world which no animal inhabits. For a man's own distinctive life shows him to be a creature as far beyond the apes as these are beyond the dinosaurs, or perhaps even the highest of the plants. For dormant or awakened in men is the power to bestow reality on many of his ideas. Pondering on some lack in his surroundings, some unsatisfied desire in himself, there occurs to him an idea of what will satisfy the desire; and labouring, he calls it into being—his cottage with its simple furnishings for use and pleasure, or something gleaming and imperishable. Men are makers, are in a large measure makers even of themselves, being creatures and creators in one. An ancient seer, not without some justification, exclaimed of men, 'Ye are gods.'

The seer, however, was but partly justified. For in man are massive contradictions. Creator though man is, he is also the most destructive of all the living beings on earth. Within the nations there stand face to face generosity and avarice; mercy and cruelty; solicitude for life, and recklessness of it; science and wildest delusions; honour and crime. And from homelands to peoples abroad there are as never in any earlier age immense networks of effort to relieve the hungry, the homeless and the sick; to share prosperity and understanding, and protection against injustice and crime; and black beside these is war waged with a magnitude and ferocity, and lasting woe beyond anything in the dreams of the insane. No description equals the sorry truth. In private life, in organizations in our domestic life, and in intercourse of peoples with one another the world over, there is this contradiction of all that is worth our respect. It threatens, it challenges. Is this godlike? It is demonic.

It is a menace, perhaps the greatest ever known. All the peoples of the world and especially those of the Occident are being shaken to their foundations by forces that threaten them with disruption—a disruption of their culture and spirit that can at best be repaired but slowly during centuries to come.

Indeed it is a manifold challenge. These forces threaten all men with immeasurable ruin, both within them and without, including the loss of confidence in their ability to cope with the powers causing this desolation. The outcome depends on the kind of response we and other peoples make to the threat, the challenge.

The manner of meeting any such challenge, as Toynbee has shown, may be of fateful consequence to peoples. For some have been invigorated by it, and summoning all that was in them, have with stout heart and will victoriously risen lastingly to a new level of life. Others so threatened have faced it feebly or even passively, and have sunk to a lower level than before.

And what is the actual response to-day of men generally to the world's peril? There is anxiety. Many are working with might and main, but as yet there is no world-wide enlightened and indomitable will to face the challenge victoriously. Many regard the whole situation as due to forces outside man, and as little to be controlled as are earthquakes or tidal waves; others see the world's turmoil due wholly to economics and to be downed by better economies. Still others hold it to be deep in human nature, and ineradicable. The fatalists are for inert acceptance. And those not fatalists are of so many minds regarding the cause and cure of what besets us that joint confident effort is well-nigh impossible. Yet this fatalism, this confusion and crossing of purposes are not warranted by the facts themselves. A concerted, intelligent labour toward success is justified by a scrutiny of the sources of the evils we must combat, and of man's ability to control these sources.

II

What then is the source of this contradiction that threatens and challenges us? And can we work far more effectively toward a preventive, a cure? If so, the work to be done is clear.

To believe that men by their very nature, that is, by their natural endowment alone, without learning and training, will grow up into true members of the community, who are free and creative individuals—this belief is utter folly. Contrary to all evidence though it is, this folly is held by many. And it is no less a folly to believe that men who are disloyal and destructive, are the only true mirrors of human nature. And a further folly is to believe that the savageries in our civilization, may be open or concealed, but they never can be uprooted. The evidence declares this to be false.

In fact, man by nature is endowed most lavishly, and yet is most incomplete. This endowment includes all the raw abilities needed for making a man of high excellence. The actual making of him is never what nature alone has done for him. But no less is there in man's natural endowment all the raw abilities for making a man ready for abhorrent acts.

The making of creators calls, not mainly for 'hands off' the child, as some would have it, but for a wise union of hands on and hands off, to steer the child gradually into working membership in a community of men. The child's native constitution with its disproportioned strength of drives, its instability of inner government, its readiness for cramping attachments, must be shaped toward full inner and outer participation in a great civilization. This is the prime requisite for important creative work, for in it all he must acquire skill in using such instruments of his craft as already exist; and for mastery he must in mind stand abreast of that craft's farthest advances thus far; he must find human assistants. But underneath all this there must be a valuing of the greater community. This valuing will be the counsellor of his originality so that he will make of the community a better habitation for the body and spirit of men.

Turning now to destroyers, some of the lesser of these are made merely by leaving them outside the field of social energies that transmute the base into the nobler metal. No child needs instruction in the art of self-interest, of destroying toys, in scratching, pulling and punching playmates. And with strength gained, dramatic effects can be had for the asking by destruction of all sorts—by pulling up a plant by the roots, by throwing a stone at a window, by setting fire to a house. To plant a rose and have it bloom, to put glass into a broken window, to build a house, is beyond the skill, the patience, the strength of the young. Neglect youth and it goes the young child's way. Thus the making of petty though not negligible destroyers is easy.

But not so the great destroyers. They come by the schooling of destroyers already far advanced, by hard labour and self-denial. They must acquire needed instruments and materials, and they may be organized in a large city, across a continent, perhaps, or even in nation after nation—as is the case with gangsters or those engaged in the illicit sale of dangerous drugs; or the traffic in women and children; or the triple conspiracy directed from a single centre that became the Second World War.

Human nature, then, is rich but desert soil waiting to be watered, tilled, planted, and husbanded through the years. Unreclaimed, the land brings forth sagebrush, and aloes; reclaimed, it yields grain and grapes and olives. Despite the neglect of the work, and failure in it, there has been notable success in many times and places. In our hands to-day are more effective means than ever before, and a sharper spur to our will for the task. Redoubled power must be put into this work for the creative effort of men, and against the destructive.

III

Our needs, both domestic and international, stand clear before us. A real need is, to turn our almost limitless abilities from the production of what we already have in abundance, or do not need at all—away from these to vital matters.

But high above these is the need to direct our powers less to the fashioning of plastic, iron and uranium, and more to the re-shaping of the raw materials of our living heritage into what is demanded of us by the present age and the ages to come. The pressure of this need is such that until it is more nearly met than it is to-day, even by our most advanced peoples, the leading nations of the world will be at once civilized and savage. There is savagery in the behaviour of civilized peoples to each other, there is within each of these civilized peoples, savage thinking, savage purposes and savage conduct of groups toward other groups, of individuals toward other individuals. And the peril is not remote that the savagery now in command in several peoples may gain a vastly wider command. The need of reclaiming the waste places in humanity calls for the stoutest effort ever made. It calls for all the inventive power that is in us.

Men have ability to meet the need; they can do the work it requires. All about us are the evidences of man's ability, of man's power of mind. There long have been scholars, it is true, who being victims of their theories deny this, holding that men's thinking, men's conscious desires and purposes take no effective part in making these things; these arise wholly from forces in the outer world, and in men's muscles, glands and nerves. And many hold that ultimately all happens by chance, and by chance alone. Does it not seem incredible that not a few men of science can look out on our dams and aqueducts, our railways and ocean liners, our libraries and universities, our sciences and arts, and say without a smile: 'Yes, but these in strict truth have not come of man's thought or desire or intention, but by such blind action as is seen in throwing dice or in flipping a coin for heads or tails.' Such a relief can be held only by men—to speak in Berkeley's manner—who have been debauched by learning.

The plain facts about us and in us, and drawn from the past by research announce that man is powerful beyond anything found in water or oil, in coal or plutonium; and further, that he has dominion over these lifeless energies, and still other energies and can compel them to do his will; commanding their help in making persons from the raw stuff of human beings and of making communities from these persons.

This is no work for specialists alone, though they will have a high place in the reclamation of human waste lands wherever found. Specialists in many a long-established science are needed, and in many an art, particularly in statecraft. But all others, too, are demanded—the learned and the ignorant, the employer and the employed, women and men, of every place and station. Each will continue his special work, but will fit it to this larger purpose. The economist in the midst of his statistics of production, costs and prices will all the while have a fraction of his mind alive to the undollared value of men. The teacher will teach the facts, but never without an eye on far more. And so the grocer, the salesman, the plumber. Artists, too, whether in line or colour, or in the magic of words and ideas, will then be restless until their talent is in accord with another art that includes their own and is above it.

IV

For is not the making of persons and a community of persons the greatest of arts? It need be no enemy of other arts, except those which destroy the spirit of man and his finest creations. Instead it would invigorate and liberate literature, painting, and music; and science and all the arts that humanely apply the discoveries of science. It would rejoice in these as the partial fulfilment of its own true purpose to create creators and to rid creators of their enemies. And many are they who are labouring to fulfil this purpose. And though imperfect in even their best results, yet magnificent through the ages has been the achievement.

Measured by the courses of the stars, however, the art is at its beginning; and for its future, any understanding of the art, such as the present study has sought, is far from enough. To knowledge of the work needed must be added desire, ardour, and the will to achieve. This addition has already been carried far. Multitudes of men who reject with indifference or disfavour the religion most potent in the west, nevertheless bear the impress of its seal upon them. These added to those who intentionally accept its guidance will be leaders and supporters in this art. And the art will lead and support them in making effective these three imperatives: To direct steadfastly, loyally, all that is in one's self into accord with what is Divine; To hold the person and the well-being of one's neighbour (and to-day all the world is neighbour) as no whit less important than one's own; And to fashion a world-wide community in which these commands govern its members.

All these imperatives, though tragically violated, are in our Western inheritance, in our brain and blood, in our conscience. The West, then, especially and inexorably, is summoned to prepare itself and the East to carry forward this worthiest of undertakings ever required of men.

INDEX

ability turns destructive, 87 ff.
acquisitiveness, its reshaping, 136
anarchy, international, 145 f.
animals, 23, 28, 118 ff.
anthropology: and artifacts, 27; on man's place, 25
Antigone, on man, 31
Argentina, 103, 143
Arnold of Rugby, 63
arts, the greatest of, 161 ff.
attachments: 135; and creative power, 79; extension of, 13 ff.; fateful, 123 f.
Augustine, 45, 54
Austria, 93, 104, 109
autarky, economic, 145

babes separated from their people, 50 f.
Bach, 56
Beethoven, 39
Belgium, 103
Bell, and the telephone, 26, 75
Berkeley Bishop, 56, 165
biologists, on man, 27
Bolivia, 103
bones of contention, 111
Booth, General, 112
brain physiology, on man's place, 25
Brazil, 103
British Commonwealth, 140
British Empire, 33
Brontës, the, 53
Browne, Sir Thomas, 161
Browning, 41, 76, 83
brute force and civilization, 29
Buddhism, 57, 77
Bunyan, 56

calculating machines, and mind, 16
Canada, 102
Canterbury Cathedral, 44
capitalism, 105 f.
Capone, Al, 'Scarface', 112
Carlyle, 75
Caucasians, their talents, 33
Cecil, Robert Lord, 13
Cellini, Benvenuto, 64
childhood, 117 f., 163 f.

chimney-sweep, 24 f.
China, 29, 32, 33, 34, 104, 109
Christianity, 63, 77, 133, 166
circles, warless and belligerent, 103 ff., 144, 148 f.
Coleridge, 74
communal mind, 96 ff.
communal ties, 36, 108, 122, 148, 153
community: and creative work, 33 f.; its character and power, 14, 130;
community of nations, need of, 140, 159
conscience, 154, 155
co-operation, 38, 138, 155 f.
Court of International Justice, 149
creative power: apprenticeship in, 50 ff.; and attachments, 79; and civilization, 41; and community, 36, 41 ff.; and destructive powers, 3, 164; and economics, 64 ff.; and politics, 66; and revolution, 62, 64 ff.; geography of, 32 ff.; illustrated, 3 ff., 6 ff., 9 ff., 12 ff., 14; in everyman, 72; indispensable for, 36 ff., 163; influenced by, 42; its many constituents, 69ff.; its misuse, 88; requires adventurous novelty, 41 f.; three regions of, 80 f.; town and countryside, 55 ff.
Curies, the, 13
curiosity, 20
Cyrano de Bergerac, 82

Damien, 13, 14
Dante, 76, 131
Darwin, 21, 41, 74, 126
defense, collective, 150
destructive power: and creative power, 3 ff., 85 ff., 110 ff., 122 ff., 133 ff., 161 ff.; conflicting explanations of, 90 ff.; redirection, cure of, 110 ff., 161 ff.; sources of, 95 ff., 102 ff.; varieties of, 87 ff.
Dickens, 78
dreams, insight in, 59

East, the, 161, 166
Economic and Social Council, 150, 159

economics and creativity, 64 ff.
Eddington, 30
Edison, 28
Einstein, 41
Emerson, 56, 75, 139
emotions: and attachments, 123; and creativity, 35; sthenic, asthenic, 76
endowment, differences in, 118 f.; man's and animals', 18; natural, its reshaping, 81 ff.
environment: man's and animals', 23 f.; man's power over it, 26; mental, 23 f.
Erasmus, 64
evolution: and human worth, 4; of man and animal, 18
excellence, requisites for, 32 ff.

family, 51, 131, 158 f.
France, 42, 93, 103, 108
Francis of Assisi, 77
Franklin, 74
Frederick the Great, 94
French Revolution, 65, 78

gains from findings, 110 ff.
genetics, 25
genius: 74; and intelligence, 69
Germany, 33, 42, 78, 93, 104, 109, 124
Giotto's Tower, 70
Gladstone, 83
government: within man, 126, 137, 138 f.; international, 152
Great Britain, 42, 102, 103, 108, 154
Great Community, the, 124
Greece, 32, 42, 127
Grotius, 44
Guatemala, 103

'Have' and 'Have-nots', 106
Hawthorne, 56
Helmholtz, 75
Hermit of the Sierra, 46 ff.
hermits, 77
Hitchcock, Albert S., 59
Hitler, 23, 33, 94, 124 f.
home, influence of, 51 ff.
Homer, 72, 76
Howard, John Galen, 70
Howison, George H., 63, 83
human conduct, various changes in, 10 ff.

human nature: 104 f., 116, 125 ff.; and domestic violence, 98; man's power over, 20; needs reshaping, 128; opposites in it, 73
human relations, in frequent violence and non-violence, 96 ff.
human sacrifice, 10
Hungary, 104

Ibsen, 76
imitation, 131
impulses and creativity, 35
incompleteness of man, 120 ff.
India, 29, 32
individuality, its contrasts, 74 ff.
inheritance: biological, 20, 104 f., 116, 125 ff., 128; social, 20 ff., 21 f., 22
insight: and sleep, 58 ff., 59 f.; and baffled effort, 58 ff.
instruction, 158 f.
interests, 75
International Labour Organization, 150, 159
international mind, how achieve it, 156 ff.
international society, 144
Iolanthe, 27
Italy, 32, 104, 109

James, Henry, 78
James, William, 51 f., 83, 84
Japan, 93, 104, 109, 124, 141
Japanese babe, 50 f.
Jews, 34, 42, 44, 57
John, St., 56
Jones, Rufus, 72

Kagawa, 83
Kalavala, 76
Kant, 56 f., 83, 133
Köhler, 19

labour, 11
Landor, Walter Savage, 137
Lao-tse, 58
law, 11, 44, 152
League of Nations, 93, 141, 144, 149, 151
Lenin, 41
Leonardo da Vinci, 37, 61
life, its four levels, 81 ff.
Lincoln, 13, 21, 51, 74, 131

Mahabarata, 71
man: and animals, 4, 5 ff., 17 ff., 20 ff., 28, 161; the amphibian, 161; an artifact and artificer, 27; contradictions in, 161 ff.; creator, 161; destroyer, 161; his freedom, 28 f.; his powers, 6, 13 ff., 26 f., 68, 72, 79 ff.; his worth, 3 ff., 4 ff., 5, 25 ff., 26 ff., 30; the making of, 161 ff.; as machine, 5, 15 ff., 16 ff.; natural and unnatural, 27 ; and universe, 29; what he transforms, 6 ff., 8 ff., 9 ff., 12 ff., 23, 29
Marx, 41
Masaryk, 54, 83
Mayas, 41
Mendel, 21
Mendelssohn, 53
Mexico, 103
Milton, 39, 69
mind: and body, 28, 29; corporate, 154 f.; international, 150; its place and freedom, 28; and physiology, 5; as powerless, 3 ff.; value of, 28
Mongoloids, 33
Moore, Kate Gordon, 71
morals, international, 146
More, Sir Thomas, 64
Mozart, 70
Muir, John, 52

nations: and brute force, 29; society of, 142 f.; success and failure within, 133 ff.
need, pressing, 164 f.
Netherlands, 103
non-violence, domestic, 99, 110
non-violence, international, 110
Norway, 103

obligations, international, 154 f.
occupation, choices of, 24
Ochs, 83
ordeals, 11
organization, international, 140 ff., 148

Palestine, 29, 32
Pasteur, 13, 14
Paul, St., 56, 76
peace: cause of, 104 ff.; where established, 102 ff.
Peary, 26
Peking, 37

Penn, 13
Permanent Court of Justice, 93
Persia, 29, 32, 92
personality, conforming or rebellious, 78, 79
persons, 161 ff.
Peru, 104
Piedmont, 104
Plato, 83
Poe, 74
Poincaré, 60 f.
population, pressure of, 106
Portugal, 103
possessions, inequality of, 106
Potters wheel, 131
power politics, 151
Prometheus, 29
Prussia, 73, 104, 109
psychologists: on man, 27; on race, 35
psychology: and human worth, 4; mass, 104 f.; peace, war, and, 104
pugnacity, 104 f., 120, 137

races, 33, 91 f.
rapacity, 20
reclamation, international, 140 ff.
reclamation of man: 158; aims of, 122 ff.; need of, 116 ff., 127 f.; ways and means of, 128 ff.
reclamation of societies, 127 f.
religion, 29, 133, 159
religion supplements science, 30
Renaissance, art in, 64
research, need of, 96
Revolt in the Desert, 82
Rome, 33, 92
Royce, 83
Ruskin, 135
Russia: 76, 78, 93, 104, 109, 124; its revolution, 65; its ruling interests, 43

Samson, 29, 78
Santa Barbara Mission, 26
Santayana, 72, 78
Satan, 79
savagery in the civilized, 164
Scandinavia, 151, 159
Schweitzer, 13, 63, 83
science: and human importance, 4 ff., 25; on mind, 3 ff.; supplemented by religion, 30

scientists on man, 15
Scott of the *Manchester Guardian*, 83
self-interest, 108, 125
services, changes in, 11 ff.
sex, 20, 73
Shakespeare, 56, 64, 76, 131
Sitwell, 129
Smuts, 13
social stability *v.* stagnation, 36
social ties: 109, 116; domestic, 95 ff.; international, 102 ff.; their power, 112
society: as changed by man, 9 ff.; international, 144; unfinished, 10
Socrates, 29, 63, 79, 83
sovereignty, 107, 144
Spain, 104
St. Marks, mosaics of, 15
steamship, its development, 40 f.
Stevenson, R. L., 78
strikes and lockouts, 91
struggle for existence, 24 f.
Sweden, 73, 103
Swedenborg, 48
Switzerland, 33, 103
sympathy, wide and narrow, 13 f., 73, 77 f.

talent: and race, 33; and war, 34 ff.; complements of, 74 ff.; creative or destructive, 78; geography of, 32 ff.
Tempest, the, on man, 31
Tennyson, 74, 83
Theophrastus, 74
Thompson, 54, 83
Thoreau, 56
Toynbee, 162
Trollope, 76
Turkey, 104, 109

Unconscious, the, 104 f.
understanding, international: 153; how achieve it, 156 ff.
United Nations, 93, 149, 159

United States: 93, 102, 103, 108, 142, 151, 154; civil war in, 87; creativity in, 33; individualism in, 46; races in, 87; violence in, 87; its ruling interests, 43
Uraguay, 103

Valentine and Orson, 116, 117
value of our search, 110 ff.
Vedic Hymns, 57
Venezuela, 103
vengeance, 10
violence: 87 ff., 135, 148; domestic, 95 ff., 110 ff.; 'explanations' of, 90 ff.; international, 102 ff., 110 ff.; international, its insult, its menace, 89
Virgil, 76
Visher, 53

Wagner, 75
war: 135, 146 f.; cause of, 92 ff., 104 ff.; civil, 92, 99, 103; and creative work, 34; enterprise against, 89; its waste, 88; a misuse of talent, 88; psychological, 89
Warless Circle, 103 ff.
wasps, 120
welfare, international, 151
West, the, and world community, 166
West, religion in, 29
Westminster, Statute of, 141
Whitman, 56
Wilde, 74
Wilhelm II, 94
Wilson, 13, 21, 83
wisdom, 132
Woolman, 13
Wordsworth, 39, 56, 69, 133

Xenophon, 34

Yerkes, 19
youth and age, and productivity, 67

For Product Safety Concerns and Information please contact our EU representative GPSR@taylorandfrancis.com
Taylor & Francis Verlag GmbH, Kaufingerstraße 24, 80331 München, Germany